Craft & Compass

SUCCESSFULLY CUSTOMIZE AND NAVIGATE YOUR FIRST YEARS AS A TEACHER

Troy Bradbury

© 2017 Troy Bradbury
All rights reserved.

ISBN: 1977883109
ISBN 13: 9781977883100
Library of Congress Control Number: 2017915528
CreateSpace Independent Publishing Platform
North Charleston, South Carolina

Dedication

To my wife, Amy, and my son, Gibson- You *are* the fire, the inspiration, and the constant that keeps me moving everyday.

"Always Moving Forward-Always Seeking Adventure"
LOVE

Acknowledgments

First and foremost I want to thank my wife Amy whose love, encouragement, and never-ending support is the reason this book was written. I couldn't have done any of this in my career without her and I might not be teaching today if it wasn't for her.

I want to thank those who helped edit this book. I am lucky enough to call them friends and colleagues, as well as great teachers in their own right! Audrey Ruoff for your first read through, edits, and helping me get over the fear of giving this book out. Allison Beers for ripping it apart and making me rebuild it better. Shannon James for all of your input while this was coming together and your thumbs up. Jamie Barkin for your never-ending encouragement and belief that people needed to read it. Alex Kinder, for your new teacher perspective and your support.

A very special thanks to Dr. Peggy Wilson whose friendship and professional support of me throughout my career as a teacher, mentor, and graduate student has been unparalleled. Thank you for taking the time to read, edit, and focus this book. Your final kick in the ass to get this out means the world to me. I look forward to working together for many years to come!

Thank you to the people who made me the teacher that I am today:

Dr. John Splaine for being the teacher I aspire to be. Your stories, ideas, inspiration, mentorship, and motivation has guided me through all these years. Dr. Joseph McCaleb, for teaching me the value of stories and storytelling in the classroom and guidance throughout all my time at UMD, and Dr. Wayne Slater for your support and sarcasm.

William Manion my first boss at ER. Your support, guidance, and friendship over the years mean the world to me.

Michelle Dunkle, for inviting me to be on professional teams that expanded my educational views and understanding of teaching. Also, for your advice throughout the years-You always chuckled at my naivete and it pushed me to be better.

Thank you to the ER English department mentor team past and present, Beth Dunbar, Allison Beers, James Miller, Lisa Yearwood, Audrey Ruoff, Barbara Leroux, Brendan Holleran, Anne Koroknay, Angela Bettick, Susan Vincent, and Mary Morris-Johnson. Your dedication, time, and commitment to giving back to this profession by working year after year with student interns (good and bad) has been inspiring, and I applaud you.

My AP Capstone partners- Alex Kinder, Dr. Marisha Wright, Brendan O'Connell, Sandra Lyles and Reginald McNeill- we have built an amazing program. I couldn't have done any of it without you. To my Principals, Dr. Sylvester Conyers and Reginald McNeill, thanks for supporting me throughout my career. Your belief in me, and the freedom you gave me in my classroom has made me the teacher I am today.

To my AP Capstone Consultant family, the Teach Plus Maryland cohort, and my Teachers for Global Classrooms Brazil colleagues and friends (Go Rucksacks!) You are some of the most dedicated and inspiring teachers I have ever met. Your students are lucky to have you and I am lucky to have worked with you.

A big thanks to the all of the former interns from ER. You helped inspire this book (whether you know it or not). And most importantly - you gave your time to this project while learning to become teachers

A special thank you to the following interns for making me a better teacher and giving your all with *our* students.

Meghan Finnegan
Christie Djordjevic
Shannon James
Jamie Barkin
Shirley Kim

The Eleanor Roosevelt high school staff and especially the English department (past and present)- Thank you for all you do and for always putting our students first.

A big 'Thank You' to my family- Emily, Susan and Bob Brutout. My sister Barbara and Tom Root, and my extended Gillfillan and Yaros family.

To my friends - thank you for your never ending support and friendship (even when you thought I was crazy for wanting to become a teacher).

Thank you to all of the students I've been lucky enough to have in my classes (and especially the ones I've travelled with) over the years. Watching you grow and learn has been the best gift a teacher can ask for.

And finally- to my first mentor, Beth Dunbar. You didn't realize what you were getting into at the time did you? Thank you for giving me my start at ER and guiding me through my student teaching (and first couple of years).

Chapter One

The Fire

I.
It starts with the FIRE.

You have to have that fire burning inside you to be a teacher.

That is the first step. The second is learning how to teach. Then you figure out how to become a teacher.

That is the difficult part- being a successful classroom teacher.

It is easy to become a mediocre teacher. We have plenty of those.

Being a teacher is more than just delivering a good lesson. It is more that just the theory that is learned in school. It is more than grading papers. Much more.

The space between finishing coursework, being an intern or student teacher, and surviving the first couple of years of teaching is long and unbelievably difficult.

That is why so many teachers leave the profession in the first five years.

Because it is difficult.

It's also the most awesome and amazing adventure.

But it is difficult.

You've probably heard the old saying-

"Those who can, do. Those who can't, teach."

Bullshit.

Those who can, do what? They excel -- become an expert at their job, and eventually they are drawn to, or hired to, or promoted to train/mentor/coach/instruct/advise/explain what they know to others. They are asked to share their expertise.

Yeah, we call that TEACHING.

Teaching is everywhere. We learn from others. It really is the world's oldest profession.

Teaching should be valued, honored, and exalted. And it is, in pretty much every field except education. It's a sad irony.

Teachers, and the teaching profession, have suffered a bad rap over the years. I've witnessed it, I've lived it, and I'm still in the game.

Those who can, teach.

Period.

Do you have that fire?

You know what I'm talking about. It starts with that something inside you that pushes you to want this. You want to change lives, to influence, to inspire ...

You want to be a teacher. You have that fire burning

Good.

Sadly, I've seen too many of those fires go out… extinguished in a short couple of years.

That's not going to be you.

Your job is to keep it burning.

II.

So what is this book about?

It's about the craft of teaching and how to navigate those first crucial years. It's about keeping the fire burning and not burning yourself out. It's about more than surviving your first years; it's about *thriving* during those years.

It is about bridging that gap between theory and practice, the gap between coursework and student teaching, and ultimately, the gap between being a pre-service teacher and an actual classroom teacher.

Teaching is a custom job.

You have to be unique – a custom package – to thrive in this environment.

Think of how you would build your own house. What would it look like? How many rooms would it have? What type of theme? What type of furniture? How would the landscaping look? All of these questions- all of that planning, the decisions you have to make before you build, during the build, and after you move in. And as some of you may know, once you own a home, you have to maintain it, upgrade it, update it constantly.

There is always work to be done on a home.

It is a very personal process. Mistakes will be made. But the outcome is amazing. And, if built right, it can last for years.

Your home often reflects who you are.

So does your teaching.

There is always work to do as a teacher- ways to update, upgrade, and make yourself the best teacher you can be.

I grow every year as a teacher. I hope I never stop.

However, I wish I knew then what I know now.

This is the book I wish I'd had when I was a novice teacher.

This book is inspired by years and years of hearing interns and first year teachers tell me they wish they had a book that could help them in those crucial first years.

A book they can refer to for advice, encouragement, and practical strategies to help them do more than just survive their first years.

It is about engagement. It's not a classroom lecture or hard fast rules.

I want you to engage with this book as you would in a conversation with me.

You can agree with it or disagree.

It is not a how-to or paint-by-numbers book. Use what you want to, or need to, and leave the rest.

Despite what some may profess, nobody has all the answers.

I certainly don't. I've made too many mistakes to count. I still make mistakes -- sometimes daily.

I've often forgotten my own advice. I've even had interns remind me of that advice when I've had a bad day… yeah, that is a great conversation!

But I have learned what has worked in my seventeen years in the classroom, teaching everything from regular classes to Advanced Placement classes and being a mentor teacher for most of those same years.

And I know what hasn't worked…

In this world of books, blogs, websites, publications, Facebook, Twitter, colleagues and thousands of "experts," it is hard to cut through all the noise to find what is going to work in the classroom.

This isn't about theory. This is about practical classroom application.

I have spent many years reading, reading and sometimes re-reading so much material that I thought would help me, and some, honestly, I knew would not help me become an effective teacher, but I read it anyway.

It has been through a lot of trial and error — practical application of all that material — that I learned what could actually help me in a room with real kids.

In the wealth of information available, there are many great nuggets, gems, and ideas that do work. That is why I wanted to collect everything I have learned in my time as a teacher and mentor that would help both new teachers and teachers trying to improve their craft.

But, let's get one thing clear. I am not trying to position myself as the ultimate expert in teaching.

I'm far from it. See the earlier mea culpa.

There is no one expert. You have to become your own expert, in your school, with your students.

Thinking, acting, and reflecting on what will serve your students best.

The problem with becoming a teacher is that you are often building your plane as you are flying it.

And you are usually alone.

And you're without all the right tools.

And the instructions are written in a different language.

Sounds like fun right?!

II.
Part of the problem is that we often teach the way we were taught.

If you had great teachers or a great mentor, then you are lucky. Even having a bad mentor can be illuminating, once you get some perspective.

Knowing what *not* to do can be great.

But most of us have good and bad teaching models subconsciously imprinted upon us throughout our years in school. But it can be difficult to distinguish the good teaching from the bad.

Whether from one teacher or multiple teachers, whether from high school or college that you liked or even disliked, you have subconsciously had a model for teaching imprinted upon you.

Your mentor during your student teaching experience had a huge impact on the way you see teaching. Was that example great, good, mediocre or bad? Could you even *tell* while you were student teaching?

Either way- good or bad, you now have a framework for teaching. Nobody is completely blank.

And often it is a combination of your own beliefs, the theory you've learned, your student teaching experience, and now your time in your own classroom that conflict with each other. Most of the time, the school you interned in isn't the same school you are teaching in. It has different rules, students, methods, classes, expectations…

That creates a bit of a problem doesn't it?

If you have never taught an upper level class while being an intern or never taught a lower level class and you are assigned one your first year as a teacher it might be a little problematic.

The learning curve is going to be pretty high.

Think back to your methods classes in college…

Remember you wrote that great lesson that everyone loved?

Did you try it with your students during the internship? Did it work during your internship? Would it work in your current class?

Probably not. It isn't a bad thing… it is part of the process.

I have seen too many lessons created for a class in college that would never work in a real classroom. Real world vs. pretend college world.

Teaching a lesson to classmates in college or teaching during your internship is not the same as teaching your first year.

Not even close. You are alone- no professor, no mentor, no one to support you if you crash and burn. Just you and your students...

This is a part of learning the craft.

You have to hone your teaching practice all the time. And most of the time, there is a battle between the conscious (and subconscious) beliefs and the actual practice you are trying to create.

It is up to you how you want to change it, improve it, or remove something from it to create harmony where there is none.

You may know something in your class works or doesn't work. But changing it requires a great deal of effort — from reflecting upon it, to developing a new idea, to actually implementing it. It is like breaking an old habit and developing a new habit. It takes time to get it ingrained.

This is the part where you have to craft and customize your practice in order to follow the compass.

III.
One of the single most important questions you can ask yourself when it comes to your craft is: "Is this working?"

Whether it is an administrative procedure or a lesson, ask yourself that question. Often.

Anybody who tells you his or her way is the best, or the only way, is not giving good advice. Smile and nod. Tell them "Thanks, that is great," and "I can't wait to try that." And then run... far, far away.

Beware of the cynical teachers who think they know everything about teaching and dictate to you what works because it is what they do.

But realize there *are* some amazing veterans out there who can help you. Find them and ask a lot of questions!

You must keep trying and keep learning about your craft.

That is what this book is about- How to customize your practice to fit you and who want to be as a teacher.

It is a tool for you to craft your practice and a compass for getting you there.

So engage with it.

This book is designed in a minimalist way on purpose.

You should write in it, take notes, scribble, doodle, and highlight. Bend the pages, dog-ear them, tear them out and tape them to your desk. Laminate them. Tattoo passages on your arm- just kidding...that might just be for me.

My dream is that I run into a teacher years from now who show me their worn, tattered, well-used copy and tell me that it has helped them be a better teacher.

I also wish that someone would show me their scribbled, dog-eared, highlighted copy and tell me it was handed down to them as a gift when they were a young teacher.

This book is what I have learned as a classroom teacher and mentor that I am compelled to share.

I hope it engages you, makes you stop and think, makes you smile, laugh, and have an "aha" moment.

I also hope it makes you question, makes you shake your head and say "No, that's not right."

Maybe it upsets you, makes you a little angry or pisses you off. That's okay.

I don't care if the feeling or reaction is positive or negative; it is a reaction that will make you think about what is being said.

I want you to try the things we discuss. Try them my way, and then try them your way. Maybe your way works better for you. Send me an email. Let me know. Let's engage in a conversation.

A colleague, who was once my intern, asked me an interesting question once while we were walking down the hall together:

"So, when did you know you were a great teacher?"

I stopped, looked at her and said, "I will let you know when that happens."

Do I think I'm a good teacher? Absolutely. Is there room for improvement? Always.

As Samuel Beckett once said, "Ever tried. Ever failed. No matter. Try again. Fail again. Fail better."

That is the foundation of teaching.

Let's focus on *progress* not perfection.

IV.
What this book isn't…

I could tell you story after story about the happenings in my classroom over the years. Kids are interesting and often hilarious. Some tales would make you laugh out loud, some would make you wonder, some would teach you, and a small few you'd find tragic. A good number are inspiring, and some exemplify why something worked or didn't. I have forgotten half of the stories I could tell.

This book isn't about all my stories.

I'm not here to tell you stories. You will accumulate plenty of your own.

This isn't about giving you some great idea, thought, maxim, whatever, and following it up with a story from a past class about student X who exemplifies this point. Sure, the story may be good, but I dislike a lot of those books. They don't speak to my situation or to me.

I am going to stay clear of student story land. I am going to focus on crafting certain skills and trying to help you navigate through the first couple of years.

Don't get me wrong; stories are an important aspect of teaching. My students know me as a storyteller. But, I want to disconnect the two and give you the straightforward, bare bones concepts I've distilled through years of practice.

I would rather give you the point I am trying to make and let you figure out how it applies to you. If it doesn't, forget it. If it does, apply it.

Simple.

Too many times we read those books, see those movies, or hear those stories about the teachers who transform lives magically. They portray themselves as teachers 24/7. Never giving up, never resting, never dealing with the other realities of life. This mythology is problematic.

They give everything… their blood, sweat, and tears… their body and soul.

They burn bright, hot and fast.

Then they burn out.

Yes, there are amazing teachers who have written books and been captured on the silver screen. Not everyone who is a teacher is going to match them. We see these stories and romanticize their work. We think we should be just like them.

But it is important to know that some of them have continued, and some have quit. I don't want to disparage any teacher who has changed lives. But it is interesting to see the ones who have burned for years and the one who burned out after just a few.

Even the fabled John Keating in *Dead Poet's Society* potentially burns out at the end of the movie, and we don't know what happens after it ends. Does he ever teach again? Does he ever regain that fire that was so inspirational? (Full disclosure: I don't care; that movie still rocks!)

This book is not about them, and it's not about romanticizing our profession or buying into the mythology.

This book is for you.

It is for those who want to keep the fire burning inside them for the long run, not for those who want to let the fire consume them and burn out.

It is about customizing your craft to help you navigate your first years as a teacher.

This is about cultivating the teacher in you while keeping hold of who you are outside of the classroom. It's about you and the teacher inside you. The person you are, the "I" and the professional, the "Teacher." You will see me refer to this idea multiple times; it's what I refer to as "I-Teacher."

So let's get a cup of coffee and find a place to sit where we can feel the sun. It is time to start the conversation.

Chapter Two

The Intent

I.
We build empires and empires fall.

We build institutions and institutions fail.

This has been true throughout the course of history. Things change, they evolve, they decay and die if they don't.

Teachers persevere. They are the history.

The world has changed more rapidly in the last 100 years than in the last 1000 years. Technology in the last twenty years has changed the very fabric of how we see the world. It has changed how we do business, how we get our information, how we socialize, even how we walk down the street.

Everything changes, evolves, and grows... But, how we teach has pretty much stayed the same for a long time.

We have been teaching our kids the same way for the last hundred years without much change, evolution, or growth.

We implemented the factory style of public schooling within the late 1800s and haven't looked back for the most part. (Thanks Sir Ken Robinson for making this clear!)

Years and years of desks and rows, of bells and memorization, teacher-centered instruction and top-down management systems have had a significant impact on our current system.

Sure, this is an oversimplification, but is it really?

Barring some technological advancements, how far have we really come in educating our students?

We have our students go through this antiquated, rusty, education model and then send them to college where some decide to become educators, and they get indoctrinated as teachers of this same model, then they are released into schools where we tell them to "inspire" students.

Really?!

Are we really changing things and meeting the needs of our students?

The problem is that we teach how we are taught. No wonder we are stuck in this cycle.

I once had a brilliant professor tell me that the hardest thing to change is something that has been institutionalized.

And here we are.

I am speaking in general terms here. I know there are a lot of schools, programs, and teachers that are changing the status quo and meeting the needs of our students.

I know there are great teachers who are more "traditional" and do amazing things with/for their students.

But, across the board, what grade can we really give ourselves?

Can't we, the "greatest nation," change, innovate, and keep up with the rest of the world?

We haven't.

We need to evolve.

The cycle needs to be broken. We need to train teachers for the 21st century the same way we are asking our students to be ready for the 21st century. We can't expect teachers to be ready for the ever-changing world of our students if they haven't been trained for it.

It makes no sense as an educational system in America to stay where we are. We need to find the answers to what works and change what doesn't work.

(Days, weeks, and months of standardized testing anyone?)

III.

This book isn't about learning to teach — you know how to teach; you learned in college.

This is about learning how to be an effective *TEACHER*.

It's about customizing your craft and having a compass to navigate your first years as a teacher in the 21st century.

IV.

You went to college and decided to become a teacher but...

How much do you know about the teaching profession?

Have you ever thought about why you are really doing this?

I mean really thought about it beyond some reflection piece your professor asked you to write?

Are you sure you want to do this? Why?

C'mon, think about it. You've read all the books. You've taken the classes. You've claimed your spot at the front of a classroom.

Now what?!

Let's look a little deeper…

Many teachers believe that when they get that first job, they are going to change lives.

They are ready! Nothing can stop them!

They tell themselves that they can reach every student. They tell themselves that they can really make a difference. They tell themselves they will be that same teacher that inspired them.

However, what they don't know may actually hurt them.

They will put in the hours, they will put up with the grading, and they will put up with administration.

They will create daily lesson plans, they will plan weeks and months ahead, and they will follow the curriculum.

They work, work, work… coming in early and leaving late.

They will buy in to the job. They will tell themselves that this is simply how it works and that they do it for the students. They do it for the kids.

They will go into debt, they will take a second job, they will wear themselves out, they will get sick, and they will cry when they see how some parents treat their kids.

They will take it because they know deep down they are doing the right thing.

That's the fire that is keeping them going.

But, why are they really doing this?

They have invested thousands of dollars and hours, if not tens of thousands, on this degree — this job — this profession.

What do they want to get out of it? Is it fulfilling? Is it the dream job they wanted?

This begs the question: why do most teachers quit within the first five years?

Look up the stats and the reports and the articles for yourself. About 50% of teachers give it up in the first five years; half of the entire teaching profession loses the flame.

What happens to their fire?

They burn out. Because it's harder than anybody really told them.

Here's what can happen, and often does happen, when many get their first job.

Now, this isn't everybody, but with almost 50% attrition in the first five years, I would say it is more common than a lot of people care to admit.

They will get hired by a school they may not know much about. They will be given the lowest level classes. They will have very little or no support. They will have to follow a curriculum framework that tells them to the minute what they are to be teaching.

They will have sign in and out of school. They will be required to submit to any and every new initiative administration hands down to them. They will have to learn (on the job) classroom management, software, hardware, student discipline, how to deal with parents, standardized testing practices and procedures, administrative bureaucracy, and school politics.

They will be evaluated by some arbitrary rubric and by a vice principal who hasn't been in the classroom in twenty years.

They will be held accountable for their students' achievement without regard for any outside factors such as poverty, home life, hunger, special needs, or past history in and out of school.

They will make almost no money, they will have to get a second job (or maybe keep that job they had in college). They will have to buy supplies for their classroom, and they most likely won't be able to live in the area in which they teach.

They may survive that first year… *that fire burns hot and bright*.

What nobody tells them is that when they survive the first year, the second can be even harder. That is the year when they may realize they can't help every kid. They realize that they have to let one, two or few more go who just don't seem to care. They realize that it is better to help 29 students achieve because they can't help all 30.

And those few they can't help — they gnaw at them every day. It hurts them. They can't understand why those few got away. They realize that their idea of helping every student isn't achievable.

But they survive.

Then in years 2-5

It doesn't get any easier. This is where the line is drawn.

The choice- the fork in the road- the path more- or less-traveled.

They must choose wisely, or that fire that drew them to teaching and sustained them that first year might start to burn them out.

Those next years are where they really start to see behind the curtain. And it's hard to cut through the extra noise of the school day that comes from outside just teaching lessons.

It starts to become a job. It starts grinding them down. It will be difficult to handle all the administrative bureaucracy and duties that come along with teaching every day.

Teaching — the actual time you spend in class delivering your lessons — is magic. It's everything else surrounding that precious time that is the problem.

Eventually, it stops being about the kids.

They may stop smiling.

They may start to get angry about all the little battles they lose with parents, with students, with administration...

They get sick of all the injustice.

They start to resent their job because it feels like a losing battle every day.

The grind wears them down.

They won't be able to help little Johnny and Janie read because they can't help them get more food in their stomachs. They won't be able to handle the hours upon hours of extra work. They won't be able to handle the extra job they have to get to make ends meet. They will hate being blamed for everything that is wrong in education. They will dislike dealing with the parents and the administration. They will despise being treated like a babysitter.

Worst of all, they will start seeing the indifference of the kids as a problem, not a challenge that has to be overcome.

They become cynical.

They quit for any number of the above reasons. They don't pay you enough for this shit.

Sound harsh?

It is.

That fire that used to drive their passion starts to engulf them. They are burning from the inside out.

They are burning out.

They have spent so much time, money, energy, emotion, and yes, even part of their soul, to do this job and it has burned them out.

They will most likely say goodbye, or worse, they just might stay because it's a job and they get paid.

Tragic.

I don't remember hearing about this before I started...

Any of your professors ever painted that picture for you?

Yeah, I don't remember that conversation in college.

And if your mentor gave you a hint of this then you probably didn't believe it. That is the idealism, the myth you are holding onto with both hands.

I remember those early days... like they were yesterday. I don't think I listened very closely to some of those people who were trying to help me.

I thought I was different. I thought that what they said didn't apply to me (although I did have a second job bartending and waiting tables).

I should have listened. I remember those first years and all the problems I had. Wow.

And yes, there were times I thought long and hard about leaving.

In all truth, there are times now that I wonder if I should leave.

It can be a constant battle depending on the year or time of year.

So I ask you again, tell me why you are doing this?

Right now. Take a minute. Get out a pen and start writing.

Why do you want to be a teacher?

What is your *why*? Ask yourself, "What do I believe and why am I doing this?"

The most important thing you can do in your career is to be very clear about your *why*.

It starts right here, right now. *Why are you doing this?*

In the book, *Body of Work*, author Pamela Slim poses a series of questions that also apply to our query here of why you want to be a teacher. Take a few minutes and answer these questions. Knowing these answers can potentially prevent you from being in the crash and burn category as a new teacher.

TAKE THE TIME TO ANSWER THESE.

> What do you value about teaching?
> What do you believe about teaching?
> Why do you believe it?
> Whom do you care deeply about serving?
> What problems do you want to solve?
> What drives you to act?

Stop reading and answer these!

Your answers matter. Your future, your success, your happiness in your career depends on your why.

When was the last time you heard of something good happening in education?

I read the news, and all I see is teachers getting blamed, finger pointing between unions, parents, and administrations, school-wide failures, political failures at the local, state and national level, and teachers who can't keep their hands and other things away from students.

Really!? This is the job you want?

Let me guess: You really want to help kids, right?

Why?

Why is it so important to you?

If you can't answer this question honestly to yourself, then throw this book into the fire... Let it burn.

Or you might burn.

I am not trying to scare you off. Please keep reading.

I just want to be clear.

You have to know what you value — what you truly believe in.

To become a teacher, you need your beliefs and values to become the armor that will protect you from everything they throw at you, the "slings and arrows..." because they will throw things, and it will hurt.

Lately, it seems that more people want teachers to fail than want them to succeed.

You will need your armor to survive at first.

At first, it is about surviving, then it is about thriving.

Keep the fire inside you and control it. Let it drive you always.

You can do this if you know your why.

There is still power in our profession.

We teach because we can.

You can keep from burning up.

You don't have to let it consume you.

You can more than survive; you can thrive.

Why do you think 50% of teachers quit? You can look up the various reasons. But, when you get down to it, some of the top reasons deal with how prepared they are when they got into the classroom and how supported they felt in their first years as a classroom teacher.

You know how to teach. But are you prepared to be a *TEACHER*?

I have kept that fire burning. It hasn't been easy over the years and some years are harder than others. But, it burns.

You have to learn how to keep that fire inside you. It's keeping that fire burning that will drive you to change lives. And your own.

I wrote this book to help… I know it would have helped me when I first started.

I know that if you decide to do this job then you can do it.

Effectively.

You can do this!

Some of the things I say may be confrontational. They are intended that way.

It may sound like I am complaining at times… I'm not.

I am being critical of the system that we have to work in everyday.

The system I am trying to change from the inside out.

The system I want to help you navigate, with a compass… not just you flying blind.

Which is what happens in schools across the country.
The status quo of the first year teacher.
This book is not about learning to teach.
This is about discovering how to be a *teacher.*

Chapter Three

The History

I.
The current system of education in America is wrought with so much criticism, turmoil, and frustration.

I get it. But, how did we get here?

It is important to know a small part of the history to understand where we have been. It is important to know because we need to know where we want to go. A change is needed for the teachers and most importantly, for the students.

We all have valid opinions and questions when it comes to education.

We all know that "here" is where we don't want to be. Toxic testing, poor policies, financial issues, teacher retention, etc.

It seems as though things don't change much even when governments change.

All we have to do is turn on the news to see some new report or a new study that lets us know that we have fallen behind the rest of the world or that we don't measure up to them.

But where did all this come from?

II.

I am sure we all took the class on the History of Education in college — or some version of it. It's the one where we learned about how public schools in America came to be.

We know that elite private schools and parochial schools dominated the early landscape of education. They were pretty much for the wealthy back then, and actually not much has changed today.

We've read about the "*New England Primer*," Noah Webster's Speller and the McGuffey Readers.

One of my personal favorites is the Massachusetts' *Old Deluder Satan law of 1647.*

This law stated that any town with fifty or more families had to hire a teacher and send their kids to school. This was essentially ensuring that kids wouldn't get together during the day and cause some form of mischief and to make sure kids learned the same morals and values. "Idle hands are the Devil's workshop."

We know the father of the American public school system was Horace Mann.

Without his influence, and others around him, the American public school system would not have a solid foundation. We have all read, studied and explored his work and how the Prussian model of common schools became embedded through his work.

We know about John Dewey and his philosophies.

The "biggest impact" award goes to John Dewey. He should also win the "philosophies that most need to be re-visited and applied" award.

But many have never heard of a contemporary of Mann's who had almost as much of an influence on the way we conduct public school today.

That man is Joseph Lancaster.

III.

While Mann did most of his work in Massachusetts, most of Lancaster's work was in New York and Pennsylvania.

Lancaster created and franchised what he called the 'Monitorial Method'. His idea of the monitorial method of schooling didn't last long but it had a tremendous impact on our current system.

His influence is still echoing through the halls of the American school system. His ghost is still present.

So where does he fit in the history of our public schools?

More on this in a minute.

First, let me ask you this question: "What is the purpose of a public school education?"

Have you ever thought about this?

What is your answer?

We will come back to that later, too.

Back to Lancaster...

Joseph Lancaster helped the New York Free School Society of the early to mid l800's develop a common school. The reasoning behind this movement was simple. As a result of mass immigration, stakeholders were concerned with the national identity, and the levels of crime and poverty. The idea was that education would be a cure-all for this new, growing society that existed below the wealthy. It would be a panacea — to socialize, bestow morality, and educate children in the basics in order to create a better middle and lower class. This panacea would be the answer to the problems manifesting in large urban areas or on the expanding western frontier.

(It was the *Old Deluder Satan law* on a larger level.)

The schools in New York didn't have a great deal of money so they needed a good way to educate the masses. Hence the monitorial system of Lancaster would be a cost efficient way to address their needs. Lancaster didn't necessarily create this model; he lifted most of it from the Prussian model, but he is credited with is widespread popularity at the time.

The first component you might recognize is the classroom set-up.

The monitorial method could educate up to 100 students at a time with one teacher at the front and more advanced row monitors who would administer the lessons from the teacher to their respective rows. It was easier to teach a large number of students in this method because the teacher could focus on the row monitors and in turn the lesson would move down to each student. This was easier and more cost effective than teaching smaller class sizes.

This model was a perfect fit for NY, and its only limitation was the size of the room. It was a perfect system to "warehouse" children in order to get them off the streets — I mean, to "educate" them.

The echo lives today. Schools around me are four grade levels and around 2800 students. I know some schools in New York and Florida are four grade levels and 4000-5000 students. It's like a small city!

The second, and more fascinating, component is the way punishments were dealt with in this model.

Punishments occurred if students were talking, wasting time, or for any other misconduct during the school day. Some faced corporal punishment and some faced something more severe.

Students were turned in by their monitors and faced punishments designed to make an example of them. This was done in order to get them to act accordingly. Sound familiar?

Here are a few of my favorites:

Classroom problems were solved by enforcing strict punishments on students. Students would be forced to have:

> Wooden logs of 4-6 pounds tied around the student's neck so they can't look around at their neighbors.

> Their legs shackled and make them walk around the room in order to tire them out.
>
> Their arms and legs shackled and then hoisted to the ceiling in a basket for everyone in the classroom to see them. This was called the "bird in the basket."
>
> If you were truant you would get a large sign that reads 'TRUANT' fastened around the neck and the student is tied to a post in the room for the day.

All of these would enforce both physical and psychological pain in order to get students to conform.

These punishments are all indicative of a system that mistrusts the student. In this system the students behave are physical abused and/or psychologically traumatized through embarrassment and humiliation. Awesome... I think I went to this high school.

I know we don't do this any more per se, so I guess we have "evolved."

Gone are the days of paddling and dunce caps. But I have witnessed the psychological traumatization in classrooms today.

Think about the rules you might have or have seen in the past when you were at school. Does any of the above resemble or echo those ideas? What about putting a student's name on the board, a student sitting in time-out, or staying after school for detention? What about a teacher verbally abusing a student?

There is a difference between confronting a student to motivate them or holding them accountable and making them feel like garbage.

Shaming students is not good practice.

Ever seen anything like these? Where should we draw the line? What kind of schools do you want to work in? What kind of classroom will you have?

Lancaster dictated every aspect of his "school" — from the size of the building and the classrooms, to how students should enter and leave the classroom, especially their behavior.

He believed that there was "A Place for Everything, and Everything in its Place."

He essentially created what we would call today a franchise model of education. It was like a school in a box-like some charter schools. These ideas mimicked the industrial nature of the time. Factories were spreading across the world during this time and Lancaster wanted to capitalize and monetize his ideas.

Education modeled the machines and factories of his time.

Sounds great… for the 1800s!

This method does not make sense for our time. And, while this system fell out of favor soon after its implementation, you can see how certain elements became institutionalized and still exist today.

The ideas of the common school movement directed by Mann and Lancaster can still be heard today: schooling to combat poverty, reduce crime, and change behavior.

Lancaster's one-size-fits-all model of education, while short-lived, was monumentally influential with regard to today's schools.

Schools are still designed in a square, students seated in rows facing the instructor, expectations about behavior, rules, ability-level grouping and punishments have driven public schools for the last 150 years.

Dewey and other reformers of the time wanted to create public schools that were different than Lancaster. He, and others, didn't feel that the industrialized model was the best for students. However, no one side won the battle and the public school system became a hybrid of both.

One hundred and fifty years later, Lancaster's ideas and voice still haunt our public schools. His large classroom sizes, his idea of teachers in the front delivering the knowledge, and his punitive measures to keep students behavior in line are a part of his legacy.

The ghost of Joseph Lancaster still walks the halls of the American public school system. His ideas about creating a public school panacea is still alive and well, sadly.

Education – "A place for everything and everything in its place."

And it worked for the time. It was unbelievably efficient, innovative and desperately needed for the time- *for the time!*

I think we can do better.

IV.

So where does that leave us today?

I ask all my interns the same question... the one I asked you earlier before I launched into the Lancaster legacy. What is the purpose of a public school education?

Did you think about it? What did you come up with?

Here are three ideas.

The clue to the first two is in the history.

First is to create good citizens. We need people to know and understand our system of government, our laws, and what makes us American. Everyone should all have the same fund of knowledge to some degree. They need certain compulsory classes even if they aren't relevant. Like an expanded citizenship test with some math and science thrown in. We need patriots.

Second, we need obedience. People need to understand the rules — spoken and unspoken — if they want to be productive members of our society. That was very important way back then when the influx of immigrants was in full swing.

(Wait — isn't that still an issue?)

We also need everyone to buy into the system we have created, the you-must-go-to-school ethos and the American way. (There is your next clue, actually.)

Finally, public schools were created in the industrial model so they churn out products called students. We need these students to be great consumers…it was all about the economics.

Historically, we produced students in a factory setting in order for them to be ready to work in a factory — this could mean an actual factory or any 9 to 5 employment. Then they would be ready to consume the products made from those same factories.

Again, it's an economic argument… create-consume-create-consume. As people make more money they consume more, hence we need more workers prepared to work for that consumption.

Schools were tasked with creating the workers that would make the products or manage the workers, then go home and consume the products they needed to look like they achieved the American dream or way of life, which then gives value to the whole system.

Patriots who follow the rules by working in factories and buying goods and services are essentially *The Middle Class*. The middle class starts coming into prominence at around the same time public schooling becomes ubiquitous.

The public school system was not designed to create the leaders we need in the public or private sector, in the business world, the factories, or Congress. Those are the elite private schools here or abroad. Look up any one of them and note the leaders of government and industry that come out of them. Amazing.

However, public schools do produce a lot of teachers... to perpetuate the cycle.

That is not to say public schools can't produce leaders. There are hundreds of examples that would dispel this argument.

So, what was the purpose of public schools?

To create good, obedient consumers who buy in to the American way of life. And to perpetuate the structure of power that keeps the economically elite, white ruling class in charge. To read more see Seth Godin's *Stop Stealing Dreams*

Again, this was great for the time. But we don't live in that time anymore. Things have changed. Drastically.

The problem is that we don't have factories in America anymore, and we have a shrinking middle class and a school to prison pipeline.

So why do we still educate like we did back then?

I once had a professor who used to say when confronted with an issue such as this: "The hardest thing to change is something that has been institutionalized."

We have been institutionalized.

So, what are we really preparing students for?

We live in a global world now.

You may be a product of the public schools, and thus you have been indoctrinated for the most part in the belief system. If you are from private school, you are a bit different but you still have some of the same Kool-Aid mustache.

Right or wrong- when you participate in the U.S. public school system, you are participating in:

> Standardized curriculums
> The ACT/SAT as a gateway to college
> Vo-Tech as less than important
> Standardized Testing
> Grades
> Bell systems and static start/end times
> Rote memorization
> Competition
> Obedience
> Punishments for behavior
> All classes for all students
> Standard grade levels
> Ability grouping
> Teachers are the problem
> Tenure
> One size fits all
> Teacher as sage
> Teacher-led management of the classroom
> School hierarchy/top down management/administration as leaders
> Brick and mortar schools
> Technology as savior

> Only the right answers are valued
> Desks in rows

The list goes on and on.

Do you believe in all these things? Is this what you are ready to buy into?

I don't really believe in a lot of these for the most part… for some, I have never believed in them. For others, I've had to re-program myself over the years by reading new studies, reading great research, and listening to those I think make sense in education.

It is hard work to continually confront my own beliefs or at least question them. I went to public and private school, here and abroad.

I also believe I can change the paradigm, or the system, while I am working in the system. For some, working outside the system is for them. There are many inside and outside that are battling for change.

Education policy and practice are often at odds. They need to come together.

However, I appreciate anyone trying to change the system for the better, no matter where or how he or she works.

I am not trying to talk you out of becoming a teacher. *I am trying to prepare you to be a teacher.*

You don't have to "buy in" to everything. You just have to establish a line in the sand between what you believe, what you don't believe, and what you want to change.

There is power in knowing how the history of education in America still affects us today.

There is power in knowing that we can change it.

It is time for an education revolution.

Chapter Four

The Craft

I.
"So, what do you do?"

That question comes up every time you meet a new person — at a friend's house, a party, a date, sitting at a bar, flying on a plane — pretty much everywhere.

We tend to define ourselves by what we do.

The author Robert Fulghum wrote a great chapter about this in one of his books about the 'standard strangers on a plane' question.

Most people define themselves by what they put on their business card. Fulghum likes to make up occupations and see where the story goes when he is confronted with this question on a plane. Pretty cool.

The artist Marcel Duchamp used to say that he was a "breather." It is what he did most of the day and was pretty good at it. Fulghum took that same idea and called himself a napper. He's really great at naps.

It is hard to tell people what you do and not launch into a huge biography.

It is hard to tell people that I am a teacher because it such a loaded term. It encompasses so much, and many people don't have a positive reaction when I say it.

Here is the typical exchange when I meet somebody new:

"So, what do you do?"

"I'm a teacher."

"Oh… that must be so hard." Or "Oh…wow…do you like it?"

What I am I supposed to say to that? What are they really looking for? Do they want me to agree? Are they expecting me to say, "It is so hard and I hate every minute of it."

But I hate that question. Because as soon as I say I'm a teacher, then the floodgates open.

Rarely does anyone ever just say, "Oh, cool. Tell me more about it."

Why?

Because many people (non-educators) think they know, that they understand, that they actually have a clue about what it means to be a teacher.

They know because their mom was a teacher or their sister is a teacher. They know because they read an article in TIME magazine, saw that movie, or simply because they went to high school that they understand what it means to be a teacher.

NO. SORRY. I DON'T THINK SO!

Think about it...

I don't know what it's like to be a chef because I have eaten in a hundred restaurants, watch *Top Chef* or the *Food Network* and get *Food and Wine* magazine delivered to my house. I know nothing of what it means to prep food, run a kitchen, manage behind the line, manage the front of the house staff, deal with the ordering, do the books, the bar, the money and so on...

To claim I have an idea about what it really takes to do all that is insulting and absurd.

But mention being a teacher...

And it seems as though everyone loves to hear and comment about the flaws and faults in our education system. Everybody has an opinion.

You know what they say about opinions, right?

I'm not always sure why people feel compelled to share their opinions about education.

Maybe it is because if I, the teacher, spout a bunch of negative b.s., it justifies the misguided notions and ideas they have about teaching and education. In the mind of the guy on the plane, if an actual teacher is complaining about the system, well then it must be messed up. It validates their beliefs.

They get to be right and will use phrases like, "Well, I was talking to this one teacher and they said... *insert stupid complaint here*..." Or "Well, I was reading this article in... and it must be the same for you, right?"

NO. Don't give them the satisfaction. Don't give them any fodder to fan the negative flames.

My wife (not a teacher) hates when people ask her what I do. When she says, "He teaches," the asking person gets that look on their face and says "Ohhh, that must be so difficult." Like it's a given that I hate my job if I teach.

So many people instantly think that if you are a teacher, you are unhappy with your job.

NO.

It is time to change that idea.

We aren't even going to talk about the money thing.

We all know it is not what it should be. It isn't why we got into this job.

The problem is that a lot of teachers talk about the bad stuff and there is bad stuff to talk about but, c'mon. Some people just love to complain about everything. Remember that rule about not ever going into the teachers lounge?

Some teachers complain incessantly. I just don't like hearing it.

How much the job sucks, the kids suck, the administration sucks, the government sucks… a myriad of "this sucks" or "that sucks".

I want to look at them and say, "Hey, maybe it's you that sucks!"

I just don't want to hear it all the time. Sometimes, when it is really warranted, sure. Otherwise, I would rather stab myself in the face with a #2 pencil. Repeatedly.

I try to never complain to strangers, acquaintances, friends… even my wife and family (well, maybe to them sometimes, but rarely).

Why?

Simple. *I chose to do this!*

It wasn't like I didn't know a lot of the problems going in. It wasn't like once I became a teacher that some mysterious curtain was pulled back and I saw all the problems. The great and powerful Oz didn't make an appearance.

I pretty much knew going in… and I *wanted* to do this.

When I don't want to do this anymore, for whatever reason, I will quit. I won't bitch. I will just stop.

It's always a choice.

Becoming a teacher wasn't really a surprise.

You would have to live in a complete bubble and be completely ignorant to not know what you are getting into. Why would you choose to do this if you didn't want to? It isn't like *Brave New World* where you are born (actually decanted) into your station and job forever.

I CHOSE TO DO THIS!

YOU CHOSE TO DO THIS!

YES!

I'll take it a step further.

I believe…

I *GET* TO DO THIS.

They pay me (a little) to do it. And, I actually smile to myself every day that I walk into the building.

Here is how I see it:

I get to hang out and talk about the things that I am inspired by and passionate about with students. My job is to get students excited about engaging in the world and learning about their place and how they can use the skills I teach them to help their lives.

It is the best job in the world.

Sure... do certain things get me down, piss me off, make me a little cynical, and sometimes get me downright angry? Absolutely! Without question! Federal, state, local policy anyone?!

But me being angry is not for some guy on a plane that thinks he knows something about being a teacher. I am not going to add to the problems currently facing the teaching profession by fanning the flames with strangers.

So here's my two cents:

If I do talk about being a teacher, I tell people I love my job.

Not in a "puppy dogs and rainbows" type of way, but realistically. Yes, I don't agree with all the policies and procedures but I bet they feel the same way about their job.

I tell them the good far, far outweighs the bad.

I tell people that my students are awesome, that teaching is fun, exciting, a challenge that only the best can do.

I am proud of what I do. I treat it like I am one of the chosen few that can actually do it. I feel like it is my duty to change people's perception of us as teachers. I treat it like Tom Sawyer painting his fence. "You could do this, if we let you. Maybe."

So, what is the point?

How do you define yourself and what you do? Are you going to buy in to the problem and be one of those complaining people? Or will you believe what we do is amazing and, just like everything else in life, has good and bad to it?

You are an artisan. I know the denotation of the word isn't exactly correct when it comes to being a teacher, but I like the metaphor. It takes time, practice, energy, and a desire to build your skills as a teacher. What do we create?

We create students. Life-long learners. College and career-ready students. Good citizens. Whatever your definition or whatever you believe the goal of education to be is what you create.

I tell the interns in my building at the end of the first meeting of the year: "This is a serious job, you have a lot of responsibility, and it is going to take a lot of time. You will be tired, you will stress out, and some of you may even cry. However, I want you to remember this one thing: It should also be fun. If you aren't having fun then you are doing it wrong and should maybe re-evaluate why you are here."

Where do you want to stand?

With those of us who "get to, choose to, and love to" or those who want to whine, complain, and hate?

II

This is like a "Choose-Your-Own-Adventure" story.

If you do choose one path then you get to go on; if you don't, your story is over, time to do something else. Some people aren't cut out to be teachers.

If you choose correctly then you will need to cultivate the two sides of you. The I and the Teacher.

Let me explain. I don't reduce who I am to one single thing. If I did, I should tell people that I am a breather like Duchamp, or a reader. It is what I do more than anything else.

In order to thrive at being a teacher, you must be able to combine and separate these two elements.

Who you are should be the same inside and outside of the classroom — to a degree. Who you are must be authentic inside and outside of the classroom.

But, who you are inside the classroom is not entirely who you are outside. What I mean is that you cannot be all consumed with being a teacher in your life outside the classroom. And you should keep some things from your personal life outside the classroom as well.

Somehow we are led to believe that being a teacher is something that has to consume our entire lives. This mythology is damaging.

But, you need to have a passion for teaching AND a passion for other things in your life.

You need to be able to shift between the teacher life and the personal life.

Life outside the classroom needs to be cultivated the same way life in the classroom is cultivated.

Often, by shifting between the personal and professional, I have come up with my best ideas about teaching. It's like the saying; "I get my best ideas in the shower." Sometimes by turning off, you are actually turning on other parts of you that can creatively solve issues you may be facing in the classroom.

III.
Profession versus Lifestyle

The hardest aspect of the job of being a teacher is dealing with the bureaucracy. When you reflect upon your day, month, semester, year, you will see so much of your time eaten away by administrative tasks that having absolutely NOTHING to do with the actual education of students.

Please see #2 pencil reference earlier.

I don't want to bore you with all the mundane tasks I have to accomplish during the day that are deemed important. They vary by school system. If you are a teacher you know what I'm talking about. If you aren't yet, you will.

In order to deal with all the garbage that you will be confronted with during your time as a teacher, you will have to become resilient.

To deal with the compression, you must decompress.

During a typical day and even during a normal class period, you are thinking about multiple things all at once...

you are multitasking on an exponential level. You have to manage the content, the personalities, the time, the delivery, the interruptions, the task, multiple learning styles, technology, and on and on… and all while thinking ahead to curriculum, and unit plans and test schedules. God forbid you are being observed that day. Whew. That is a lot going on all at once.

You need to decompress after doing this all day.

How are you going to do this? What is it that is going to let you separate your life in school and outside?

Do you have a hobby? Do you have a side job? Do you have something to occupy your mind outside of teaching?

I kept my hobbies and the job that helped me get through college during my first five years of teaching.

I played in an original band that rehearsed a couple of times a week and often played gigs on weekends. I also worked as a bartender and server in a small upscale restaurant. When I found the time, I also played golf with friends.

All the extra-curricular activities that people tell you that you should have in high school and college shouldn't go away once you get a job.

The band allowed me to get out all my creative energy, some aggression, and I got to spend time with some of my best friends.

I was a bartender on Friday nights and was a server on Saturdays. This allowed me to interact with other people, it allowed me to completely separate myself from teaching, and it gave me extra money. I joked early on that I would make more money on Friday and Saturday nights at the restaurant than I would make in a week of teaching. (True story.)

Golf was something that helped me get away from everything else. I've been playing since I was twelve, and it allows me to just be and see other friends.

About friends... Keep as many as possible from different aspects of your life... Whatever works for you. You will make friends at school. They will be fun, and you can hang out after school, go to happy hour, or have weekly poker games at someone's house.

Here is the danger. If you surround yourself with people who you work with, at some point, you will talk about school. It is inevitable. Work comes up. That is fine if you only hang out once in a while. The problem arises when they become your main circle of friends. Then you become immersed in teaching, or aspects of teaching, on a consistent basis.

The one thing I know about most people, especially teachers working in the same building, is that they talk about a lot of what happens day in and out. Ever meet anyone who worked together and didn't talk constantly about his or her job?

It can be tiring to carry all of that with you every day.

Don't get me wrong. It is important to have work friends. I actually play golf more often than not with a few people from work. It is great.

I go to lunch with some colleagues, go to their houses for parties, or go out for dinner.

I travel on EF Tours with other teachers. I love my school friends. The same way I love my old friends, my bar friends, my band friends, etc.

But it is important to diversify. It can save you from being swallowed up.

Teaching can be extremely time consuming. You will have to make it a point to keep hanging out with your old friends or make time for new friends.

Schedule time to join a club, attend a meet up, play kickball or another sport, something... just make sure you are balancing the two.

If you need an extra job to make ends meet, which is often the case for new teachers, then find one that will work with your schedule during the year and in the summer. Working in the restaurant business is perfect.

However, I would advise against working in the same area as your school. There is nothing worse than waiting on a student and the family; it completely messes with the dynamics. I refused to do it and would give away that table the few times it happened.

I always reserved Friday night and Saturday for myself, my hobbies, my friends, work — ultimately, what I wanted to do.

Sunday was spent preparing for school — prep, planning, grading, ironing, etc. The days don't matter. It is carving out the time during the weekend to decompress.

A little side note about grading — Make sure when you do have to grade at home that you are in a situation where you can enjoy it as much as possible. I like to grade while sitting on my favorite chair, or sitting outside, cup of coffee next to me and my favorite music playing.

That is what works for me.

This is something you need to think about but need to apply it in a way that works for you. Where are you happiest or the most comfortable? Is it on the couch in your house or apartment? Do you have a local coffee shop hangout?

I used to have a college professor come into my bar when I was setting up for the night, and he would grade a few papers while eating and having a soda. Once he was done he would reward himself with a beer and a conversation.

It worked for him.

I try not to grade at home anymore.

I have restructured my daily work habits to grade everything at school. I go in a little earlier, stay a little later, only have lunch with my colleagues a couple of days a during the week, in order to get it done.

Once I had kids, I decided that when I was home, it was family time. This doesn't always work but I get about 90% done at school now, whereas before it was 90% at home.

You need to cultivate a persona, or maintain a persona, outside of teaching. You need to let that persona grow and learn the same way you tell your students to do the same.

We talk about students being life-long learners and experiencing the world. You need to do the same.

This job will wear you out physically. I mean it.

You will be on your feet most of the time, talking, and thinking. It isn't physically hard work but it is mentally and physically connected and exhausting.

If you aren't healthy, it makes the job twice as hard.

And you will find that most good teachers never want to take the day off. It can actually be twice as hard to take a day off. You will see.

I hate taking days off. If for nothing else, I don't get to see my students that day, and they are awesome. I feel like I missed something.

Staying healthy is a priority.

You know your body and what you need to do. I always have coffee and water next to me. I eat as healthy as possible during the day and save the junk food for the weekend. I also make sure I have snacks in case I start to feel my blood sugar drop.

I noticed once during my third year of teaching that I was getting irritable right before 8th period and would snap at my last class. I ate a granola bar every day for a week before that class and whoosh… a completely different class.

Amazing what a little reflection and problem solving will do. [Also notice that I didn't think it was the class's fault. I looked at myself first.]

I exercise regularly— Yoga anyone? Anyone want to go kayaking or stand up paddle boarding? I also meditate.

Does it impact your teaching?

Absolutely.

Pretty much everything you do or experience outside of class will have an impact on you in the classroom.

My advice as a teacher is to travel. Travel near, far, just go, go, go and often. You will be a better teacher for it.

I actually like traveling with other teachers. There are a lot of programs out there for teachers to secure travel to different countries to learn a variety of things. The teachers I have met traveling have been some of the best people and teachers. They are the epitome of what and who a teacher should be.

They seemed to have learned everything that I am trying to relate to you. Rarely do they ever complain about teaching. They may bitch a little about the b.s. politics, but these teachers are energetic and influential, and their excitement is contagious.

I dare you to take a teaching trip and not come back with a whole new perspective about the world, your classroom and your place in education. It is transformative and necessary.

Here is an example of what not to do to decompress:

Bitch about teaching on Facebook, Twitter, on a blog, or in a bar to others (happy hour with colleagues is different).

Don't ever bitch to your class about having to teach. It's unprofessional. Just don't do it.

It's ok to complain about bad educational policies but you don't want you students to ever think that you don't want to be with them in the classroom.

Do not work at a job that revolves around education... test prep, tutoring, etc., until you have more experience. Never in your first five years.

Go ahead as soon as you start thriving.

The last thing you should never do as a teacher...

Do not ever, ever, ever, bring your personal baggage into the classroom. The time you have with those students is sacred.

Do you hear me? It is sacred.

They deserve you and the best you can do every day. No question.

Here is what I tell my interns—take it how you want:

"I don't care about the problems in your personal life. I don't care if your boyfriend or girlfriend is mad at you because you can't commit. I don't care if they cheated on you or just broke up with you. I don't care if you just got fired, ran out of money, or your car broke down again. I don't care if your dog ran away, your parents threw you out, or your aunt Millie is sick. When it is time to teach, you are ON."

YOU ARE ON!

Let me clarify before you call me an ass and toss this book.

I do care about you and I will listen and try to help with anything you have going on that is creating a problem for you… when class is over or when the school day is done. I've helped my interns with family problems, relationship issues, and even car troubles. I've sent them home and covered for them when they have been sick, or a family member has passed. I have given them rides to school; I even gave one of my interns a coffee maker because she said she was spending too much money at Starbucks.

I see it as part of my job as a good mentor and a good person.

But, when it is time to teach, you better be prepared and ready to go. You should be energized and excited to cover what is happening that day.

Even if you have to fake it. Fake it until you make it.

We have an old saying in the restaurant business: "When the show is on, you are on the floor." That means you are ready to go and doing your job when it is time.

It is your job as a professional.

It is your job as a teacher.

It goes back to the old belief: Students will not remember what you taught them, but how you made them feel.

If you are there every day, you are present, and they know you want to help them, they will respond in a positive manner.

You will be a teacher.

IV.

You have to be inspired, inside the classroom and outside.

What inspires you? Why?

Are you excited to teach everyday?

You need to be honest about who you are and what you can and can't do.

How well do you know your subject? How good of a classroom manager are you?

How do you deliver your content? How do you talk to your students?

How do you handle it when you don't have an answer to a question?

How are your students experiencing what you are doing?

How do you ask for help?

You must find a mentor in your building that can help you with your craft. It can be someone in your department or just an experienced teacher who isn't burnt out.

Learn from them, what works and what doesn't.

Learn what to do and maybe what not to do. Don't be afraid to ask questions.

Too often we think that once we are teachers, we are experts and don't need help or are too embarrassed to ask. Too often we are so isolated in our rooms that we don't get time to ask for help.

I know one of the most troublesome aspects of teaching is that we don't get the opportunity to observe other great teachers.

Identify the great teachers in your building and find time to talk to them or go observe them during your planning period. If you don't know whom to see, ask the kids. They know.

Go see them. Don't be afraid. And ask them questions!

Getting a degree in education and getting a job as a teacher isn't the end of your journey; it is only the beginning.

You had access to experts in college, and you often asked them questions. Why not do the same at your job?

Think about this: How would you teach somebody one of your hobbies?

Where would you start?

What are you good at? Think about it...

What do you do for fun, or for a hobby? How would you teach me how to do that if I didn't know?

How would you teach me soccer, golf, football? How about chess, poker, tic-tac-toe?

How about cooking, playing the guitar, taking a photo?

How would you do it? Sit down and map it out.

Right now you want me to give you an example. The problem is that how I would do it is most likely different than you would. Not wrong, just different.

I play golf, cook, and play guitar. If you asked me to teach you these things I would probably do it differently than you would.

I would do what works for me. How I have crafted my instruction in these things is different.

For golf, I start with the grip (if you are a late teenager or adult); with a child I would just give them a club and let them swing. It's two different approaches on the same topic.

For guitar, I would start with learning strumming and power chords. You might start with standard chords.

For cooking: This is interesting because I learned from a chef, so I would teach you the same way he taught me (we teach how we were taught)... how to hold a knife and mise-en-place (preparing everything first).

Your grandmother might have taught you how to make something, and you would start with that first.

The point is you have to figure out how to best deliver your instruction to students.

How does it work best for you? How to customize it to who you are.

That could be a lot of trial and error with positive and negative outcomes, some interesting reflection, and actively thinking about what is working.

If you are doing this, then you are custom crafting your abilities.

Welcome — you are becoming a teacher.

Chapter Five

The Community

I.
Classroom management is the single most important aspect of being a teacher.

It can make you or break you.

I've seen it break more than a few new teachers; it's not pretty. In fact, most of the teachers who can't manage their classrooms leave sooner rather than later. It is one of the top five reasons teachers quit in the first five years.

The idea is simple.

Learn to manage your classroom or just hang a sign on yourself that says, "I quit!"

Classroom management is so important that more than a few colleges don't even have a class for their pre-service teachers.

Yeah, you read that correctly. It's not a typo. They don't offer a classroom management class as part of the undergrad or grad experience.

It's that important and some places don't offer a class in it? Yep.

You may have talked about it *in a class* but was it an entire class on the subject?

When one of the top reasons new teachers leave the profession is due to problems within the classroom, don't you think more time should be devoted to it?

So how do you learn?

Most teachers say they learned on job: Trial by fire. Sink or swim. Thrown to the wolves.

That sounds like a great idea... NOT!

It is like putting a kid behind the steering wheel of a car and telling them to drive without getting into an accident because they have sat in the passenger seat and observed someone else driving for years.

Yeah, that makes sense. Totally.

How does this happen? How is it even possible?

Usually it goes like this: In some teaching methods class, they mention that you have to have classroom rules. They tell you about setting standards and expectations for the kids to follow. They tell you about modeling the school rules, or to take those of your mentor teachers, or my favorite theory, "let the kids decide."

None of these is going to work well.

Maybe you got a book or a handout — something about "effective teaching strategies" or "classroom management that really works." Maybe you got a pamphlet about the "first days of school" that had simple, effective rules for the first semester.

Maybe you got advice from your county, district, or school during that "New Teacher Week" like "Just be stern" and "Don't be too nice" or my personal favorite, "Don't smile until the holiday break."

Yep. That should do it.

Please don't get stuck on the Internet searching for things like "surviving the first days of school." You will be overwhelmed with information, most of which won't be truly effective for your class.

Try not to take anything with the words "surviving" or "tips and/or tricks" too seriously. It's okay to read them and synthesize a few for what you need. Everyone does that. But another teacher's system may not work for you entirely.

This is a custom job. Remember that from the beginning?

By the way, I dislike the term *classroom management*. It goes back to that whole industry/factory thing we talked about with Lancaster in the history chapter. It reminds me too much of a teacher-centered classroom where the teacher is the controlling and students must obey.

I prefer the idea of a *classroom community* or *classroom environment*.

We don't manage or control our students — Too Orwellian for me.

We have relationships with our students. I like this much better- I think Dewey would agree.

But I understand that good classroom management leads to creating a community in the classroom. Classroom management doesn't have to be heavy handed and authoritarian; it can be simply a way to have students meet certain expectations for a positive learning environment.

It's not about managing a classroom or students with a heavy hand. It's about building a community, an environment, establishing expectations that help create and foster relationships. Sounds all hooey and touchy-feely.

And I'm all in.

You've been told that you must wield an iron fist in your classroom. You must set the bar high, and don't let students get away with anything.

This is your classroom and you dictate how things run. You are in control.

(But are you really?!)

Being the authority figure is class is important, but not being a dictator.

See the difference in language there? Creating, building, fostering... vs. wield, get away with, dictate, control.

It makes a difference.

I could give you a bunch of stories of the trials and tribulations in my classroom.

Nope. Not gonna do it. It wouldn't help you.

Have I had classes that were difficult? Sure. Students who were difficult? Check. Have I struggled? Oh yeah!

Has it taken me years to develop and create my classroom community?

Yes.

Do I have to be flexible and adjust every year to meet the needs of specific classes? Yes.

That is how you adapt and achieve a community. Not every class is the same or needs the same from you as the teacher.

Some classes need more direction and authority over them than others. Sometimes one class can take all of your energy. It can take all you have to simply keep everyone together and productive.

Adapt your expectations to each class as needed.

But do you have to be Sisyphus constantly pushing his rock up the hill? No. There are ways to create community in your classroom that don't require a pound of flesh offered up as payment.

You want to be simple, transparent, and effective.

II.

Two things are important when it comes to your classroom: How you see it and how your students see it.

Simply put: If your class is created in a negative context, then your students will reciprocate or mirror that negativity.

Teacher X: "My students are horrible, they just suck and every day is a struggle!"

Teacher Y: "Why? What happens?"

Teacher X: "Most of them are late every day and I have to yell at them for that, none of them are prepared, they don't care, and someone is always talking. I am constantly telling them to be quiet. They don't follow the rules. They are so disrespectful!"

I've witnessed this first hand- multiple times.

Look in the mirror. Frustration mirrors frustration.

If their actions frustrate you and you take it out on them...well... it becomes a cycle.

If you walk into your classroom and immediately feel, believe, know, that you have bad students, then what do you think is going to happen?

If you talk down to them every day, how are they going to act? How are they going to treat you?

Here is another thing I want you to think about. When I talk to people about being a teacher, they often reply with, "Wow, that must be hard... the kids these days are so bad..."

Here is my standard reply: "No — I've never had a bad kid. I've had students with problems or who behave poorly in class, some more than others, but I don't know any bad kids."

I do believe that kids are inherently good. Some just have problems in some areas. Some problems we understand, some we don't. Some problems we can relate to, others we can't. We can't always help our students but we can always listen.

Are you listening to your students, both their verbal and non-verbal actions in the class?

Think about it... They communicate to you both verbally and non-verbally. What are they saying? What are they not saying? How are they sitting? What does their body language tell you?

Understanding this is critical.

It makes a huge difference.

Another question-

What do you believe about your students?

This is all about perception. How you see things can be an issue.

Try to visit a classroom with a negative learning environment. Notice when and where the teacher is condescending, reprimanding, or yelling at the students. Take note of the reasons why. What words and phrases are being used? How does the teacher stand and look at the students?

How do the students look? What are the students doing back to the teacher? Are they mirroring the same attitudes and actions of the teacher? Are they scared? Are they intimidated? How are they acting?

Then go see the opposite.

Notice what works and what doesn't --- take notes!

Maybe if things were set up differently then maybe the action could be different. Maybe then, the re-action would be different.

Then adapt and implement in your own room.
Customize your approach and watch what happens!

III.

What do you want your class to look like?

Think about your favorite class of all time. Now reverse-engineer that class from the teacher or professor's point of view. What were the rules or the expectations, the policies and practices, what was the environment like? How did the teacher treat you? Talk to you? How do you think that teacher would have handled a student that was a problem?

Think about it. Copy it. Model it.

Here is another question-

What biases do you have about your students or the school population? You must confront these. You must face them, understand them, and check them at the door.

Check them at the door!

If you believe any stereotypes about students, then you must look at them and see if that influences your classroom community.

Do the smart kids sit up front? Do the bad kids sit in the back? Who do you teach to (who are you looking at)? Do you expect more of a white student or an African-American? Do you expect too much from an Asian or Indian student? Do you get along with the girls or boys better? How do you deal with sexual identity?

Keep thinking to yourself about all the negative and positive stereotypes about kids as kids and kids as learners in your room.

Are you consciously or unconsciously acting on these in the community of your classroom?

You need to answer the questions honestly because it is critical to who you are as a teacher and your classroom community. Don't give me the "I see all people equally" line because it is bs.

Are you one of those teachers who looks at their roster before school starts and finds the teacher who had them last year in order to know who is going to be a potential problem?

Yeah, I've done that too. But I work hard to not let that influence how I treat them the first week of class. I try to let my students dictate how they want to be treated based on my experience with them in my classroom. Not how another teacher viewed them.

I do use other teacher information to let me know about certain students who have a "history" and I can use that to help me create a different connection with them or how to serve them better in my room.

If these ideas are uncomfortable or you are not well versed in this area you need to read up on diversity issues in the classroom. It is important!

If you teach in a predominately minority area and you are white then you need to read up on the research! It makes a difference.

IV.

Think about the concept of respect.

What does it mean to you? How do you define it? What needs to happen in order for you to feel disrespected? Where is the line in the sand?

If you haven't thought about this or are able to define it for yourself, you are in for a ride.

You need to take a minute and really think about this.

You need to write it down and let your students know where that line is.

You want/demand respect because you are the adult/teacher. But when you don't check your bias or when you talk down to them constantly because you have certain beliefs about them, then what do you expect? Where does the mutual respect begin?

The point is that some kids today have a different notion of what respect is and think they deserve it for doing nothing. This is a belief — you have a belief as well. What is your belief?

They don't want to give you respect because they really don't have any for themselves. We all know the psychology behind it. But what matters is that you don't take anything students do in a negative way in class personally.

If you think that students talking while you are teaching is disrespectful, you are going to be disrespected on a daily basis. How do you think it would feel and what do you think it would do to your mental health if you spent most of your time during the day in a state of feeling disrespected?

See teacher X above. It makes you angry, cynical, and tired. A burnout candidate

Wherever you draw the line, you can be pretty sure a student will cross it someday — or every day— if you don't understand it.

Here are some of mine…Let's look at what is disrespectful to me.

Late to class? *Nope.*

Talking during class? *No.*

Eating? *No way.*

Sleeping? *Aww, isn't that cute.*

Passing notes? *Good luck— put it on my desk— I need lunch entertainment!*

Texting or looking at a phone? *Nice— put it on my desk We'll talk later.*

Cheating? *I'm disappointed in you. But let's figure out why you are cheating.*

"This class is stupid!" *Why? Please try to explain what you don't understand.*

"Fuck you!" *Ok. You can leave. I will see you later to discuss with Admin.*

None of these make me feel disrespected.

I don't necessarily like these behaviors but I don't take them personally and I don't feel disrespected by them.

Honestly, there isn't much you can say in my class to me that I would find totally disrespectful.

My job is to find out why they are displaying this behavior and what is happening in the class. Is it their behavior that needs to change? Or is it my behavior that needs modifying? Maybe it's the way I perceive the situation.

I find that most of these issues are with the student personally. They are a result of some external or internal force in their lives that is causing this action.

None of these are done to me personally. I need to figure out how to address the student and the issue in a positive way. Not just punish them.

Also, I get to choose how I feel when I am in school. Although it *has* happened, I try not to let a student affect my day in a negative way, if at all possible. If it happens, and again, it has happened, I try not to take it home.

Usually, it happens with students I don't know in the hallway doing something when they should be in class, and I call them on it, and they react negatively.

Let me say that again. Respect and disrespect is a personal thing. If you let what students do in your room affect you in a negative way and take it personally, then you may have a hard time.

Don't take it personally. This isn't easy, but it is necessary.

Not easy at all… but important!

V.
Creating classroom community is about creating an environment that doesn't need managing but is a cooperative

place of learning for both the students and the teacher. It is place where students feel safe to be authentically who they are without any fear and where you can be your authentic self as a teacher.

A classroom that is engaged is a community that excels.

It is about setting clear expectations for both student behavior and teacher behavior. Yes, I said teacher behavior. They both need to be communicated to students. It is a two-way street. They need to know what you expect of them and what you expect of yourself. This creates a dialogue. Dialogue creates a sense of place and belonging. Community.

If you give them your best, they will give you their best.

For instance—

I have thirty-one classroom expectations. I cover every single aspect I can think of that students may encounter in my class. From exact essay guidelines, to how work should be turned in, plagiarism, daily behavior (some school rules here), eating policy, dress code, and even a little about belief systems.

My first expectation is that "The past doesn't equal the future." I think I stole that from Anthony Robbins. Anyway, that is the first thing on my list. It tells them right away that I don't really care about what happened in other classes, whether you like this subject, whether you think you are good at this subject, or any discipline problems they may have had in past. I don't care. "WE" start today.

It sets the tone. It's a paradigm shift. It's a belief. It makes me confront my bias and their own assumptions about what can be accomplished in my class.

I explain my expectations for them academically and personally. I go so far as to tell them how to act in the outside world, and even into my expectation of how they should treat a substitute teacher. (Mess with the sub and you will go down in flames, hard and fast with the fullest extent of any punishment I can think of that makes your life miserable. Handwritten copy of Romeo and Juliet, anyone?)

Side Note:

Subs have a hard, often thankless job, and I need them. I take personal days, I take golf team days, and I travel. I need them, and my students will treat them properly. Subs say they love my classes because my classes treat them with respect and do their work. That doesn't mean they don't get talkative or do all of their work. What it means is that they don't make the sub's life miserable for that period. And I tell my students the next day that I appreciate how they acted when I was absent. It shows them that I am paying attention, and they are given credit for meeting my expectations.

I even explain to students my pet peeves. You know the little things that drive me bonkers. Tapping pens… ughh…. Stop it now! Sounds stupid, but it aggravates me. They need to know that so I don't snap at them when they do it unconsciously.

I also explain that I will try to accommodate anything they need if they are polite. I will be polite to them. I say things like -"Please open to page…" "Tonight please watch…" "Thanks for turning in your papers on time…"

I expect them to be polite as well; it is non-negotiable. "Please", "thank you", and "sorry for the interruption" when they are late to class goes a long way.

By the way- I have been late to class (usually my intern is in the room, so I am not breaking the rules) due to meeting with another adult or talking to a student about an issue. When this happens I will apologize to my class for being late. The same way I expect them to apologize.

I also stay as neutral as possible. I do not tell them what political party I follow, my personal beliefs on hot button issues, or my religion. I suggest you do the same.

All of this sets a tone. It's important.

I say "we" a lot in class. "Today we are going to look at…" "We can either do this or that…what do you want to do?" I give them choices because it gives them the illusion of democracy. Either choice is a way I want to direct them, it's a topic I want to cover. It is about creating agency.

When student feel they have agency, they listen. They contribute. They are a community.

Each of these provides structure for students. Students need structure and to be aware of what is going to happen in class. No surprises. No bullshit to get distracted.

After we go through each expectation in class, almost ad nauseum, I require them to take home my thirty-one expectations and go over each one with their parent. They both then have to sign that they have read and understand each of them.

If I have to get little Janie or Johnny in trouble for "breaking the rules," then I have documentation stating that both the student and the parent know the expectations. Saves my ass. But with that said… I have never had a parent push back against these expectations.

In fact, I originally developed 40 or so after my first couple of years of teaching. I tested each of them with my students. We whittled them down to thirty-one, kid tested, kid approved. I have used this list ever since.

VI.
Let's talk about the first week of school.

I know a good number of teachers who start teaching as soon as possible. Day one: "Welcome and here are the rules on a handout." Day two: "Open your book to page 1."

Whew… That's quick.

I don't start "teaching" until the second week of school, a good 4-5 days after the first day. My first week is about introducing the class to me, to each other, covering the overview of the class, learning names, and setting expectations for the year. Getting to know them a bit.

I get to spend an entire school year with my students. I want to know about them and I want them to know about me a bit. I want them to understand what I expect of them and what they will have to do to contribute to the class.

I ask students about their interests in school and outside. You will be amazed at what you will learn about them. You can have it on a worksheet or just have a class discussion.

The first week is spent talking TO them, WITH them. Not talking down to them.

Some people (other teachers and administration) will say you don't have enough time in the school year to start the second week. They think taking an entire week to cover the expectations, learn names, have discussions about interests, and create a sense of community is wasting time.

But let me ask you...

How much time is wasted throughout the year dealing with issues that could have been avoided if you had taken the time in the beginning? I know that taking a little extra time in the beginning pays dividends. It allows for the class to run smoothly throughout the year with minimal distractions. How much time and mental energy would that save?

VII.

If you do have issues — scratch that — *when* you have issues in your class, understanding how to resolve them is just as important as setting expectations.

You need to have a toolkit, a "go to" method for handling anything that comes up.

I try to keep it as simple as possible.

I resolve issues by first trying to eliminate the behavior that I feel is a problem. I do this by getting students' attention away from whatever is going on and putting the focus on me. Then I simply tell the student to stop the behavior because it is distracting the others in the class. If they cannot do that then they can leave to see their administrator.

I will always meet with them after class (no matter what happens) and have a conversation about the who/what/where/when/why and how about the problem and what can we do to resolve this issue. This usually curbs the behavior and life goes on the next day.

I do not get administration involved unless the student chooses to because it usually isn't absolutely necessary. I'd rather get to the bottom of the issue with the student and resolve it together. Students like having a chance to deal with me rather than admin.

Once in a while a student might do something that justifies being sent straight to administration. I just tell them to go and I will check on them later. Then we have the same talk.

Suspension is the worst. It takes them away from class and does not change the behavior. Then they fall behind, and it creates more work for you.

In-school suspension isn't much better, but it can work if done properly.

I also don't involve parents unless I have to. Some parents only hear from teachers when their kids are in trouble. Some parents only hear negative things about their kids.

I've found that asking students if they want their parents called about their behavior often stops the behavior from happening in the future. If I have to call, I will. But even then I try to tell the parents what I like about their child or what their child does well in my class and then talk about the behavior that needs to change.

I am trying to resolve the issue the student is having. I want to confront it head on and get some clarity. If I have done what I have tried do accomplish with building a relationship and creating a sense of community in the class, then the students know I am trying to help them and the class. They have always been more apt to talk and resolve the issues.

This takes trial and error. If you are looking out for your students and are really trying to help them learn, this is a process you want to customize for yourself. Creating relationships with students helps with behavior issues. Most of the time the "problem student" is reaching out and looking for somebody who cares.

You will develop an intuition about these types of situations, and it will serve you well. And you have to follow through with what you tell the student, or you will lose all you've worked to build.

VIII.
Here are your rules.

Be authentic. Students will respect that and think it's cool.

Don't confuse this with them thinking you are cool. To them you aren't; and why would you want to be cool to a teenager?

Treat them with respect but keep in mind the teacher and the students are not equal. You are the teacher and an adult. They are students and teenagers.

We as the teachers guide or lead the class.

If you have a desperate need to be liked then you need to become a rock star, start a cult, or become a superhero.

Being a teacher isn't about becoming friends with your students or having them adore you because you are cool. It isn't about your self-esteem. If you are liked by your students, great. It is nice to be liked, but it is not required. Generate self-esteem elsewhere.

IX.
Getting away from the concept of "classroom management" and into "classroom community" is not that difficult. It just goes against the status quo or the normal paradigm.

You can rule your class with an iron fist. It is possible, and it can work. But more often than not it fails.

Some might assume a credibility issue with me concerning this topic, as I am a male and over 6 feet tall. I am seen as intimidating to people because of my size.

Let me tell you from experience the best "classroom managers" I have ever seen were women who were shorter than 5'7".

Why?

They had clear expectations, and they followed through. They cared about their students and their students' learning.

Simple; transparent; effective.

It does not matter whether you are male or female, short or tall. The concepts here work.

I tell my students the old Al Capone quote, "Don't mistake my kindness for weakness. I am kind to everyone, but when someone is unkind to me, weak is not what you are going to remember about me."

Compassion and empathy are not weaknesses when it comes to teaching. They are strengths to be utilized to make your classroom community a place of learning and understanding.

A classroom community that is engaged is a wonderful place. That is the goal. That is being a teacher.

Chapter Six

The Delivery

I.

What was your favorite story as a child? Do you remember? I'll bet you do. That one story that you begged for every night. You just couldn't go to sleep without hearing it.

Jump forward…

What is your favorite book as an adult? The one that lit you on fire and made you see the world differently?

Shift gears…

What is your favorite personal story? You know the one that always comes up when you and your closest friends are hanging out reminiscing. "Hey remember the time…"

And…

What about your personal history? That one story you tell when people you've recently met start asking questions. "Where are you from?"

We tell stories. We hear stories. We watch stories.

We are made up of stories.

Stories make us human.

They are the string that connects us, the bind that makes us stronger, and they are what live on after we are gone.

We are stories.

Think about all the media we are exposed to all day long. It is all stories, packaged and presented in myriad ways but essentially the same.

Book-Movies-Music-Art-TV-Social Media-The Internet-Gaming...

Fiction...Non-Fiction...

So what is the point?

It is all a story.

Life is a story.

II.

How does this fit into teaching? How do stories fit into the classroom?

Ahh... Glad you asked.

This is the second of three main components of teaching. The first was how to create community in your classroom (classroom management).

This component is about storytelling and delivery of instruction.

How you talk to your students and what you tell them is just as vital as the content of your classroom.

Take a step back for a second.

In the last chapter we spoke about the classroom community. The interactions you have with your students create emotions and they create a tone.

How you speak to your students and what you tell them is just as important.

The tone you take when speaking to your students can outweigh what you are teaching.

Think about a classroom where negativity hangs over everything. Do you think anyone is really learning in that type of classroom?

While what you are teaching is vital, creating a positive tone in the class helps the message stick. It goes deeper and stays longer.

This is simple marketing. Create an emotion, repeat that emotion, anchor it, and reinforce it. Message received.

Think about all of those annoying TV commercials, the ones with the silly, stupid songs. They work don't they? You remember them and their products even if you don't use them.

What about the commercial about all the lonely, abused, and neglected animals in shelters. The one with the really sad song playing in the background and the despair in the voice of the narrator… you want to go save all of those animals, don't you?

Just as soon as you wipe the tears away.

It works because it is effective and it is effective because it works.

Think of branding or brand loyalty. It works. To the tune of billions of dollars spent every year. The entire advertising business is built on creating emotions and connecting them to a product.

(I am typing this on my Apple MacBook Air and answering a text on my iPhone, all while listening to iTunes.) Sucker.

How about this...

If you go to a restaurant and they treat you poorly and/or give you horrible service would you go back if the food was good but not great?

Or

What if the staff and the experience were extremely positive? They went out of their way to give you a great experience but the food was ok but not bad.

Where would you re-visit?

My friends and I always say (and we have all been in the restaurant business for years) that we can forgive bad food, but not bad service. (But this has caveats as well.)

What if your classroom were like a review on Yelp? Or students could review and comment on a class like they do on products coming from Amazon.

Have you ever read some of the comments on these sites? How did it affect your decision?

Have you seen the ones out there that rate high school and college teachers? They can be brutal. I suggest being careful if you go there.

However, getting honest feedback is great but you should get it directly from your students- not from anonymous reviews on a website. College professors get surveyed at the end of every course, why wouldn't you want the same.

Let's say, hypothetically, that your content is good. (I know it is.) How would your students rate the "service" they are getting? I'm not talking about how cool they think you are because you are young, dress well, listen to the same music as they do, watch the same shows…

But,

How would they rate your content, your attitude, your ability to teach, to make the content relevant, to help them understand new concepts and refine their old knowledge. Would they say your class is hard but fair? How would they rate your ability to grade? Your ability to discuss? A the end of the day what do they think about you as a teacher?

I am talking about making your classroom a place that students look forward to coming to every day because they know the way you deliver your instruction is good, you connect with them, and the content is great.

What if that looked like your classroom?

How do you feel about the restaurant that has amazing food that provides a great experience at the same time? I've been to a few of those places. I will always spend my money there.

I know what you may be thinking. Teaching is not a like a restaurant and teaching students isn't a "customer service experience."

Really!?

Because in my most recent evaluation, of which I am sure that I am not alone, the students had an opportunity to evaluate me, and it counted on my overall score.

Yep.

In some areas this is tied to tenure, advancement ($), or bonuses.

You might want to read that last line again.

Maybe you would prefer the idea that everything in life revolves around the concept of sales. Does that work?

Aren't you really trying to sell something (yourself, your content area, a belief) to your students?

So how do you do that effectively?

Tell a story.

III.

Think about your favorite classes from the past. What do they have in common?

Most people forget most of the content they learned, but their favorite teachers made them *feel* something.

They don't remember exactly what they learned but they loved going to that class because it felt good.

They were treated well; they were helped; they were held to a higher standard; the teacher was tough but fair; he/she cared.

The best class you ever had was?

Why?

How did it make you feel?

Would you want your students to feel the same as you did about that class?

I know I would.

IV.

Your delivery of instruction can be simply put as your "style."

What is your style of teaching? Each of us must cultivate that within our classrooms. No one way is correct, but there are many wrong ways.

This is just as important as any other aspect of teaching. Your style defines you, it becomes part of who you are, and it becomes your reputation in school.

Think about that for a while.

How do you want to be known around school? What do you think the students say, the other teachers, the administration, and the parents?

All of the best teachers in my school have various styles. More importantly, the ones I know outside of school act in a very similar manner as they do in school.

They are authentic.

They have crafted and customized the teacher side of their persona, but ultimately it is an extension of who they really are.

They are authentic to themselves. They know themselves.

Students can smell fake.

Trying to be someone you are not because a professor, a mentor, or fellow colleague told you to do X (what worked for them) will get you in trouble.

Students can also smell fear.

And fear can paralyze you in a classroom.

If you are uncomfortable with what you are teaching, you aren't sure if you're capable, or if you are nervous about your "management" of the class, the students can read that, and they will do anything and everything in their power to throw you off of your game.

Whatever it is that rattles you, they will repeat the same thing, day in and day out because they know you have lost confidence and are afraid.

Either of those in your classroom will sink you for that year. You better make the next year better. Reflect and adjust.

If you don't and it becomes a pattern, it is time to find another school or another job. Students will tell everyone how to get under your skin and it will spread like a disease. It can ruin you.

See you on the other side…

You need to find ways to address your confidence and fear- what aspect of class do you feel confident in?

What fears do you have?

Figure out exactly what it is you do well and what you don't do well.

Once you are clear on what you need to get help with, then seek it out from those in the building you respect.

Don't fall into the trap that if you aren't great at everything, then you are failing at being a teacher. All of us have strengths and weaknesses. You have to capitalize on your strengths and address your weaknesses.

I am confident in my ability to create a classroom community and a highly engaged classroom, among other things.

I am not the best writing teacher in my building. If I have questions about writing I have multiple teachers I can seek out for help- and I do.

Why *wouldn't* I go to them for help with writing instruction? They are awesome and willing to help. I don't feel that I have to be great at everything.

Seek help from the awesome teachers in your building. If you know a teacher in your department is great at a particular aspect of teaching, then go get advice. If you know a teacher in another department is great at creating engagement, then go ask.

It doesn't make you less of a teacher... It actually makes you a better teacher!

Imagine taking all of that expert advice from different teachers and customizing for your classroom and teaching?

Think of the potential effect it would have?

Awesome.

Elite athletes have multiple coaches... why shouldn't you?

V.

I am a storyteller.

That is how I teach. I tell personal stories, historical stories, anecdotes, and random bits of information on a daily basis.

It is part of who I am. It is how my students know me.

Years ago, I noticed that students who wrote evaluations of my class always talked about the stories I told and how it was the favorite part of the class.

I have cultivated that aspect of my teaching and make sure I have continued with that practice.

However,

I know teachers who are strictly business- and that works for them because it is who they are.

Who are you?

Remember I told you at the beginning that you teach how you were taught, for better or worse.

Decide who you want to be in the classroom.

Spend time crafting who you are in the classroom. Don't just mimic your mentor teacher. What if you are nothing alike?

Think about your mentor, what you liked and what you didn't like. Write it down and decide what you want to use for yourself and what you want to throw away.

Don't just accept it.

Custom craft it.

Look at multiple teachers in your building, or think about the teachers you had at the university level and in high school. What qualities and attributes did you like in them? List them and think about what you can use.

Likewise, think about all the bad teachers you had and list their qualities.

Decide not to be like them.

Actors, comedians, professional speakers, spoken word performers, poets, musicians all have to craft who they are onstage. They have a style, a cadence to their voice, a tone, an attitude, and a method to do what they do.

Redd Foxx influenced Richard Pryor, who did the same for Eddie Murphy. Eddie then influenced Chris Rock and Dave Chappelle. You can see the influence in each of them. They are different comedians and have different styles, but you can see the influence, and it works for them.

The Blues influenced The Stones and The Beatles, who then influenced Led Zeppelin and Black Sabbath, who influenced… pretty much everyone else in rock.

Ever see the original Batman movies — Keaton, Kilmer, Clooney? Then watch Christian Bale. Same character. Different styles.

What is your style?

I draw my influences from a multitude of places, but I can narrow it down to three professors from college… and a few others.

The first one made me think by challenging me with questions over and over until I started making sense.

The second was a real professional storyteller who wove amazing tales into his class.

The third was a funny, sarcastic professor who told little anecdotes throughout his class.

Outside of academia was...

The multi-faceted, punk rock, spoken word artist and author Henry Rollins also influenced me. The delivery of his content had a huge impact on me, and I still watch and listen to his DVDs and CDs (I started with his cassette tapes - it's been a long time).

I would also say I have a little dose of Anthony Robbins in there as well. You have to keep them motivated, right? Ever see him talk to a crowd? Amazing energy and his content is top notch.

Each of these teachers tells stories intertwined with their content. It works for them and it works for me.

They also are energetic "on stage;" they don't sit at or behind a table or desk. They get up and engage. They incorporate their audience in the story. When you are enthusiastic about what you are talking about, it can be contagious.

Ever see those infomercials where the person is acting a little too enthusiastic about their product? Ever want to buy that product just to see if it really is as good as they say. You know you do or maybe it's just me...but I suspect I'm not alone.

Some of our students have been so used to the boring and bland delivery of their teachers that they are thirsting for some enthusiasm.

Bueller? Bueller?

The great teachers also want feedback from their audience, and they get it because their audience is engaged with them. They are engrossed and along for the ride. Ever see a great performance, a concert or comedian who owns the crowd? Awesome.

These teachers can gauge whether the audience is with them and understands what they are saying.

This is vital in the classroom.

These teachers also use humor in their work. People (students) who are laughing are also engaged.

How you tell your stories, what stories you want to tell, and how deep you want to go is up to you, but people connect to things they can identify with.

Use what you know: Your life, your hobbies, funny happenings in your life and the world, interesting happenings with friends, travel stories, random knowledge about a story you read, trivia, interesting times you failed but learned something.

The possibilities are endless. It is up to you to make the connection to your lessons on a daily basis.

However, they shouldn't be contrived or fake.

The reason they work is because stories are transformative. All of our emotions can be expressed and felt through storytelling.

That is why the written word has been and is so influential throughout history -- think Shakespeare, the Bible. That is why the movie business is worth billions a year.

Think about *Star Wars* or the *Marvel* Franchise!

That is also why music touches everyone — insert your favorite artists here. Why do you like them?

Because they speak to you!

Teachers need to use and capitalize on story telling to engage their classes.

It helps the sale. It helps with the customer experience. It helps make you a better teacher.

VI.

I think about delivering content in a way that connects to students in a relevant and real way. I try to connect things to the world they live in today.

Something relevant to the lives of a student is an important connection. I know that your content can often dictate how you link these up but think hard and make it relevant.

I can link almost anything to the modern superhero movies. Pretty much each one of them has all the elements I need to teach students, and most everyone has seen the movies or knows the stories.

This is also true of the *Harry Potter* movies, *The Hunger Games* movies, and *Star Wars* movies. These are teaching tools. It is your job to figure out how to use them to your benefit.

VII.

Along with the verbal delivery, the non-verbal is just as important.

How do you dress every day at school? What do you wear? What image are you portraying, consciously and unconsciously? What are you communicating to your class with the way you look, stand, and say?

(More on how to dress and what you should or shouldn't wear later.)

All of these are part of who you are.

A colleague of mine (who is awesome) once said, "I have never taught a class without wearing a tie!"

I replied to him, "I have never taught a class wearing a tie!"

(Not entirely true; I wore one when I was student teaching and being observed by my university supervisor and one day on Crazy Day.)

But really, I don't wear a tie when I am teaching. Ever. It is not who I am.

Some might say this doesn't matter, and we could debate for hours why it does or doesn't. The bottom line — it does matter.

How you look in class, how and what you say, and your mannerisms, all matter.

You are being judged by your students and the people evaluating you on a daily basis.

What are these things saying about you and your teaching?

This is why you should make videos of yourself teaching your classes. Watch them and analyze yourself. You should also look at your lesson, and the student engagement, during that time.

Be honest and see where you are with your style. What are the positives, what are the negatives, and how can you capitalize on both?

You have to do this in order to graduate from your teaching program, and you may again if you become Nationally Board Certified.

It is eye opening, it is helpful, and it can be very powerful!

IX.

Take risks with your teaching. Sometimes you and your lesson will fail. Sometimes it will be amazing. If you are being authentic, then no matter what, you will learn how to be a better teacher.

You need to be actively engaged with your class when you are delivering your lesson for the day.

I call this *active teaching*.

What is active teaching?

It is where you are thinking about everything (being proactive and reactive) concerning what is going on in your class during the lesson.

You have so much to pay attention to, anticipate, and make decisions about every class, every day.

You are thinking about:

> Your students: individual needs (IEPs, 504s) and collectively.
> The lesson: today, yesterday and tomorrow outcomes.

Managing the time.

Managing disruptions: from school alarms to announcements.

Behavior: Address positive and negative- individually/collectively.

Engagement.

What you need them to do tomorrow.

What they did yesterday and scaffolding for today.

Developing good questions.

Calling on students from multiple areas of the class: not just the "hands up"

Gauging for understanding: who's got it and who doesn't, and why?

Connecting to the real world.

Anticipating potential student questions.

Being sure you have some answers.

The homework.

Attendance: who is here, who isn't (for how long), why?

Student safety.

Maybe even what is for lunch.

And what errands you have to run on your way home!

When you can wrap yourself around all of this and move around inside and outside of it daily... you are *actively teaching.*

You are a teacher.

When you can do all this and be flexible and adjust to whatever may come your way, then you are doing what I call active teaching.

When you are an active teacher you can approach and engage each class the way that is most beneficial to them. You tailor the instruction to each class so they have the best environment in which to learn.

Each class you have is a different entity; they move differently, they think differently, they come to class with a different fund of knowledge, and so they must be treated accordingly.

It doesn't matter if it's the same class you teach in different periods or different classes in the same grade level. You could have any variation and the simple fact is that each class is different because the students act, interact, and react differently with you.

You have to adjust to the students in each class; and yes, the class must adjust to you as well, to some degree, but my point is that you drive the instruction and you can manipulate it how you want. To the benefit of the class!

When you are actively teaching your class, you develop intuitiveness about your craft. That will develop and deepen throughout the years making you, crafting you, into a master teacher.

X.
I call good teaching practice in the classroom *The Long Conversation*.

It is about asking questions and looking for answers. The best thing you can do is ask more questions.

Question students and question yourself.

The best question you can ask is "Why?" The second best question is "What if?"

Try it for yourself and try it with your students.

Ask them why they believe what they do. If you ask a question and a student answers it, the follow up is, "Why do you believe that?" Make them justify their answers.

Then ask the class a follow up question to the first, or an extension of the "why" question… "What if we looked at it this way?"

Push them. Make them push you back.

Good teaching is about teacher AND student engagement.

It's about developing teacher and student driven inquiry around topics that are interesting, practical and motivating.

It's about confronting beliefs, having a vision, researching, practicing skill sets, discussions, stories, application of knowledge, and a good many laughs.

It is about crafting how you deliver yourself as a teacher.

How you deliver your instruction becomes the story of you as a teacher.

Chapter Seven

The Content

I.
During the First World War, Henry Ford sued a newspaper for calling him ignorant in terms of general knowledge in multiple op-ed pieces. He took them to court for libel. In the trial he took the stand and was asked multiple questions about history to prove that he didn't have general knowledge about the world and his only knowledge was specialized about the car business. He eventually tired of the questions and told the lawyer that he had a button on his desk that he could push to summon one of his aides who could answer or find out the answer to any question he needed answered.

Ford stated "...why should I clutter up my mind with general knowledge, for the purpose of being able to answer questions, when I have men around me who can supply any knowledge I require?"

Badass...

Yeah, Ford won the lawsuit.

So… answer these questions:

How many feet in a mile, or how many cups in a quart, or how big is an acre?

How about naming the first five presidents, the year the Civil War started, or when the civil rights act was signed?

(Cue game show music)

Did you answer them?

You know these facts from high school, right? You memorized all of them. Or you don't know all of them but I'll bet you know where to look to get the answer.

The answer in the 21st century is simple. The Internet… right? Or "I think I have an app for that!"

Anything you need to know is all right there in the Internet, your phone, your tablet, and your computer…

Why memorize everything, anything? Right?

You knew some, or all, of the answers because they somehow matter to you. But think about your students. Does most of what they have to memorize in school matter to them? Is it relevant? Or is it just information for the sake of information?

I think you know the answer to that.

Einstein was once asked how many feet are in a mile. Einstein's reply was "I don't know, why should I fill my brain with facts I can find in two minutes in any standard reference book?"

Exactly!

Ford knew it. Einstein knew it. Why don't we seem to get it in school?

I believe that content in the traditional sense is dead.

I believe that the way we have been teaching content in school is old, tired, antiquated, outdated, and ultimately damaging to our students.

If you don't believe me, you haven't been paying attention to the current research out there. Check out the Tony Wagner's work. It might convince you.

It is time for skills-based learning. Learning for the 21st century.

II.

In the 21st century, content is dead.

Stay with me… this will be clear soon.

It's time to stop teaching facts that really don't matter.

It's time to stop having kids take tests based on what they have memorized.

In high school, I was asked to memorize the classic "To be or not to be" soliloquy from Hamlet. Yeah, failed that one. I got about ten lines in, paused, and walked away.

That failure affected my grade. And I am currently a literature teacher!

I majored in English literature in college. I even thought about getting a Master's in Shakespearean literature.

Guess what I never had to do in college or in my job? Memorize a damn soliloquy!

It is a useless task for a silly grade!

III.

It is time to change the paradigm.

The delivery of content is not teaching.

It's telling.

Standing in front of a bunch of people telling them information is not teaching.

It's a lecture.

Having them write down every last word you say in your lecture and then testing them later is also not teaching.

It's punishment.

Remember your classes in college that were lecture based?

I do.

I was usually bored, slumped down in my sleep, drawing in the margins, wondering if I was going to actually be tested on what was being said or if it was just a re-hash of a chapter in the book.

Actually, I was wondering what was I was going to have for dinner and if I needed to do laundry.

I also remember getting lectures from my parents and other authority figures. I don't remember them being very positive. They may have thought so, but I know I didn't, because they usually aren't.

(And how do you feel when the "lecturer" is an Ed professor who is explaining in the "lecture" that you shouldn't "lecture" in your classes because that is not teaching.)

Yeah, that happened more than once.

It is time to move on, move forward, and move up. The future is now. You are the catalyst.

IV.

Let's examine this further.

Content is simply "telling" in its most basic form and requires the student to memorize information. It is transferring "knowledge" from the teacher to the student. The student then transfers that same knowledge back to the teacher on a test that then is assigned a grade.

So whoever has the best memory or can cram the night before the test is the best student? That seems to leave out a lot of students who may not be great at this.

Where is the application of what they learned? Where is the problem solving?

Even worse…

The student then derives self-worth or value on what grade they get.

They only care about the information they are being tested on.

There is part of the problem.

Here is the other…

Students just want the answers because they are going to be tested on that exact answer.

I can't even tell you how many times I have asked a question to my classes that they don't know and they get frustrated and just ask for the answer. They really don't even try. They actually say "just tell us the answer!" Really?!

All they really care about is the information that is going to be on the test.

You (your school, district, state or federal government) are going to give them a test that is going to have that answer on it, and they want the information.

That is what is important, right? They need the good grades to make honor roll, to make their parents happy, to get into college, to make them feel like they have learned something useful.

And we need the data!

Then we sit back and wonder why our students aren't curious, are lacking imagination, and can't think their way out of a wet paper bag.

This is not the fault of our students! We have trained them this way! Most of us were trained this way in our own schools. We are just echoing. Perpetuating the status quo.

This isn't what was intended all the way back when Socrates was teaching... but it is where we are now.

From in-class quizzes and end-of-unit tests that are simple recall to the bane of modern education —the standardized test — it is all about memorizing that suggests knowing and data.

No child left... "actually ready for college or the future."

I am not going to get off on a rant here about testing or standardized testing. I don't necessarily believe they are all bad. (The PISA test? It tests creativity and how students apply what they know. Interested? Read Amanda Ripley's great book The Smartest Students in the World.)

Most tests have a design problem. They are designed for our students to simply remember the answers. They actually don't test what they know. They test what they can remember.

Good students remember. Bad students don't. Are we testing their knowledge or just their memory?

We "tell" them in class and then make them sit silently for the test.

When they pass, we exclaim "Great! --- We did our job!"

All we did is teach some of them how to pass the test we gave them.

When they fail, we remediate them in the same fashion that didn't work before. Then, if they continue to fail we give them a project that is easier so they can pass.

To begin with, why didn't we give them the project first? It could be alternative way to take the same test.

Then, why are we lowering the standards with the project? Shouldn't we raise them?

I don't have a problem with quizzes or tests in class, for the most part.

I just think they should be used as a way for students to apply what they have learned in a specific way.

I also don't think they should be punitive. A test for students should never be a "gotcha." That is absurd.

Ask your students what happens after a test. They resoundingly say that they forget what they have learned. The knowledge was there just to take the test.

Is this really what we want in schools?

It is a passive model that actually stifles what we are really trying to foster in children.

This model also creates self-esteem problems in students. It creates grade grubbing and students who believe they are somehow "less than" other students because they have a lower g.p.a.

It creates cookie-cutter students who can achieve if they learn the rules and can capitalize on applying those rules: listen, memorize, regurgitate, and repeat.

Success!

Right.

It penalizes anyone who can't conform. It hurts students psychologically and socially. It crushes entrepreneurialism, innovation, and individuality.

What do we really want from our students?

Why do we congratulate the student who has memorized the content in school and belittle the person who doesn't?

Are the "successful" students worth more? History would beg to differ, especially in the world of technology and innovation.

Why do we place more value on the student who gets an A in chemistry or algebra and not the student who can rebuild a car engine or build a house?

What are we really accomplishing?

V.

We all know the stories about the real innovators of the world. We laude them when we hear about their ideas and inventions, we call them geniuses, and we revere them when their ideas and products become intertwined in our lives. We use their stories as positive examples.

But do we want our students to really be like them?

Most of these people didn't do well in traditional school. They dropped out of college. Some came from money, some didn't. They take huge risks that go against the norm. They couldn't and can't perform in the box we place them in, so they create their own box.

We definitely don't want to encourage kids who aren't doing well in school to drop out. I am sure that for every "innovative leader" who dropped out of school, there are thousands who did the same who we never hear from again.

Why? What was the difference in these two kinds of kids?

We need to redefine what schools are teaching to be more inclusive. We don't need to change things completely; we just need a model that is more flexible and adaptable to what our students need.

We need to adjust, adapt new ideas and change the paradigm.

Content is dead in the 21st century.

Or is it?

VI.

Let's get two things clear before we go too far down this rabbit hole.

First, YOU need content knowledge.

Second, YOUR students need to have certain content knowledge.

You need to know your content area. Period.

I told you to stay with me... I know that content isn't entirely dead.

None of what I say in this chapter is supposed to negate the fact that as teachers we need to know our content areas. We do need to have specialized knowledge like Henry Ford and Albert Einstein.

But we don't need to "teach/test" knowledge within our content that isn't important. You can't just get a degree in teaching and be lacking in your content area. It is vital that you have a thorough knowledge about your subject matter. You can't teach geometry if you don't have a thorough understanding of it. Same with the rest of math, science, English, and the list doesn't end. Ever been taught a foreign language by a teacher that doesn't speak it fluently? That would be insane.

If you are teaching a story or a time in history, you need to have read and reviewed it before teaching it to the students. You need to anticipate what questions your students might ask. You need to look up additional resources or links on the web.

I am not advocating that we shouldn't be teaching content to our students. It just shouldn't be the only thing we teach.

I also believe wholeheartedly that our students need to have a certain depth of knowledge about specific content.

They should know simple math concepts; they should know what century the First World War was in, what the branches of government are supposed to do, who wrote Hamlet.

They really should have a clue where India, Italy and Indiana are on a map, at least the correct continent.

They should know about biology, chemistry, and engineering concepts. Environmental science, absolutely. World languages? You bet, but it should be taught at elementary school and reinforced in high school (then they should travel to that country).

And they should read multiple fiction and non-fiction books, poetry, speeches, plays, etc. The written word in any form should not be scary.

We need to know specific content areas so we can teach them.

THEN, in addition to the content, we want them to develop and ask questions ABOUT these topics; not just sit back and passively "learn" them.

Then we teach them how to investigate these ideas on a deeper level and apply what they know.

This allows them to question, analyze, and synthesize. It allows the student to make mistakes and learn how to adjust, adapt, and capitalize on their effort.

It allows them autonomy in their learning.

Then we ask them to collaborate with others or work independently to present what they have learned to us. They get to teach us!

We want them to grow. We should evaluate their growth, not just the end result.

If we evaluate how they have progressed throughout their topic or their work, we will see them grow. That growth is the learning we are striving for. We don't need them to be perfect.

Progress not perfection.

If all the students in your class get an A on a test, wouldn't you question how valid the test is? The same if all kids got a D.

What if you get the bell curve on the test? Is the test valid? Good question.

What if on the next test, the same bell curve happens for the most part. The same students got the same grade give or take a few points. How do you view that?

Traditionally, we would say some kids get it and others don't, or that class is right on track.

But... If the same students are getting the same grades then where or how is that student growing? Are you challenging the student enough?

Can you differentiate their learning on a personal level or a whole class level?

Skills-based or project-based learning allows for this.

We can no longer afford to be the "sage on the stage" or the "expert." We need to be working with our students as mentors, coaches, and as co-learners.

Imagine that; we model the life-long learning process for them.

They learn to apply their knowledge. They imagine, discover, write, create, and build...

They get to capitalize on the content they have learned in order to improve the skills they have.

The process is amazing.

But what skills do we need to be teaching alongside the content we have?

VII.
The skills.

The skills needed in the increasingly diverse and connected world aren't a mystery. Type in 21st century learner or skills into your browser and a whole "gaggle" of info comes up.

The skills needed by learners in today's world are circular and recursive.

Here they are in no particular order-

> Students need to be engaged thinkers, have an entrepreneurial spirit, and be an ethical citizen.
> They need literacy and numeracy skills.
> They need to be able to think critically, solve problems, be creative, and have digital and media literacy.
> They need good communication, collaboration and leadership skills.
> They should be socially responsible, culturally, globally, and environmentally aware.
> They should be self-directed learners with imagination and self-management tools.
> They should enjoy learning and reading.
> They need to be able to adapt.

That is a tall order, but most of these skills are embedded within others. These skills go hand in hand with content areas.

They are not taught separately but within the content we are already trained to teach.

VIII.
Knowledge is power, right?
No, it isn't.

Access to knowledge is power and application of knowledge is power.

Just knowing something doesn't give one power.

If that were true then the most intelligent people on the planet would have the most power. We know that is not true!

What skills are students leaving school with? Can they transfer what they know to new situations?

I tell my students they should work in the restaurant business at least once in their lives. It teaches so many skills that are important to making it in the world. People who work in the business are more savvy, they can talk to people; they can sell; they multitask; they have to deal with people on multiple levels; they work under high stress situations; their work equals their tips; they work long hours; they have to deal with money; they have to have great customer service skills.

These are all *skills*.

About the only content they need to know working in the business is memorizing the food, wine, beer, and health codes about safe food handling. The rest are all skills.

Skills that pay the bills. (Yes, I went there.) I've never heard of "content that pays the bills."

If you aren't teaching all, some, or any of these skills, are you really giving your students what they need to be ready for college (in any form), the military, or the global world?

What are we really doing to our students?

I know content still drives most everything in schools. It is part of the history of schools and we do what we know. It made sense in the 18th, 19th, and even the 20th century, but now with the ubiquitous nature of computers and access to the internet, it is really irresponsible to be teaching content the way we have for as long as we have.

The title "content is dead" isn't completely true, but I got your attention. We need to have content and we need to be teaching skills too.

We need to have a combination of both.

I know we are moving that way… new courses, new textbooks…inquiry based learning…project-based learning, but I am not hearing the call loudly enough. It is still on the fringe.

We need to have an honest conversation about the intentions of school and a balance between teaching our students skills and the content that really matters.

IX.

So where do you start if you are stuck in a school that isn't trying to change, grow, or innovate?

The best place to start teaching these skills is within your content area. Some of the most important skills you can teach a student are how to read critically and annotate text. Next is the teaching of, or the reinforcement of, writing skills.

If these are not your strongest suits, then create that interdisciplinary connection with an English teacher in your building who is like-minded, then collaborate. Work toward a common good.

Explain to students what you are trying to do and why. They will get it, and you will be giving your students a great gift.

So how does this all fit, skills and content? How do you plan for it?

Make sure you have learned or learn now the best way for you to plan. I plan smaller units that build to another. But I don't plan every minute of every day. I do weekly planning. I need to be flexible. I need to make sure I am adapting to what my students need during that week before I can move on. Some of my plans for the week become my plans for two weeks.

I need to design, adjust, re-adjust and implement.

I like the framework of *Understanding by Design* by Wiggins and McTighe. I like to go from big picture and questions to skills, then the content that delivers that skill.

Skills need to be scaffolded. You remember that term right? Vygotsky.

You can't expect students to write a great paper if you haven't taught them how to write.

We learn one piece, then another, then another, and build knowledge. What we could once only do with the help of others, we can now do ourselves.

I like the simplified model of "I Do-We Do-You Do." I show them how to do something, then we do it together, and then they do it on their own (or in groups).

I remember an old wood shop teacher I had in 7th grade. We were tasked with building a birdhouse. He showed us a finished birdhouse for us to examine. He then went about showing us how to build one. Then he worked with a few students to build one together. Then we were put into teams of two where we helped each other build our own birdhouses. He didn't evaluate the end result; he watched the process, how we solved the problems we faced, how we worked with the machines, how we helped each other.

It didn't occur to me at the time that he was giving me one of the greatest teaching lessons of my life. Actually it didn't occur to me until I was well into teaching, and I was looking for an example to give to an intern.

This system works for the teaching of skills. It creates autonomous learners who are confident and self-directed.

Then you can give the students formative and summative assessments that actually assess how students grow and apply what they know.

Then ask questions that students need to answer to justify how they know they learned and what they believe.

Then make them write a reflection on their learning process.

It works!

Project based learning is where we need to be now and in the future. The schools that are doing this have students who are thriving! You can look them up (High Tech High).

Side note…

Don't be afraid to ask your students the "why" question. I am not afraid to ask my students nor should my students be afraid to ask me.

I ask my students to consistently justify their ideas, reasons, and beliefs. They do this both verbally and in written form. They can do this after investigating text over time, or they can do it with a cold reading.

They are asked to identify, summarize, and evaluate arguments in texts, speeches, and debates and in various forms of media.

These are the types of assessment that really help students learn. They know where they are, what they need, and where they need to go.

It reinforces the learning process, gives them autonomy and ultimately, places the responsibility on them for their own education.

It makes what we are teaching relevant to students. They see the practical application and internalize the information. They can build their knowledge toward a goal.

X.

Teaching is really about asking questions and having access to content. It should inspire conversation, inquiry, and engagement.

Active Teaching and *The Long Conversation*.

The most important question you can ask is "why."

Little kids do this all the time. Ad nauseam. Where does this go as we age? Why don't our older students or even the adults around us ask this question?

The answer my students give: Fear of reprimand by the teacher.

It is the most important question we can ask and we (teachers and students) should ask it often... and expect an answer.

XI.

It is time to change the paradigm. It is time to kill content-based teaching as we know it in schools today. We need to fuse both content and skills-based learning in order to serve our students.

Focus on developing skills in your students because you want students to engage with the world and not just accept the status quo.

Teach them these skills and the desire to learn more about their world and the world outside.

It will give them the ability to see multiple perspectives including their own and others.

It will give them the awareness they need about their place in the world.

It will give them more choices and access.

It will allow them to defend what they have learned and why they believe what they believe.

It will help them to connect to information, concepts, and to others in a way that is new, exciting and current.

This is teaching for the 21st century. Are you preparing students for the world of yesterday, today, or what will come tomorrow?

Being a *teacher* means putting your students needs first.

The shift from a traditional teaching style (content-based) to a hybrid of skills-based and content-based is a difficult task. The longer a teacher has been in the game the harder it is to reverse that thinking.

I know this first hand as a College Board Teacher Consultant. I have helped train new teachers every summer for the AP Seminar class since the its first year. It is one half of the AP Capstone program along with the AP Research class. I teach/or have taught both classes and was the a part of the 16 school pilot program that became AP Capstone.

Chapter Eight

The Custom Classroom

I.

If you could completely design your classroom what would it look like? What would be in it? How would you set it up?

These are important factors that should not be overlooked. I have seen many new teachers simply set up their room the same way their mentor teachers did.

My question is always the same: Did you really think about your room or did you just follow your mentor's lead?

During student teaching you were forced to work in the confines of how your mentor set up the room. You had to work in that framework, so you became comfortable with it.

Ask yourself: Is this how I really want my room or am I just comfortable with it because it is all I know?

During my student teaching, I made my classes change the desks in the first five minutes of class. I didn't like the set up so I had them move in to a circle. Sure, it took a couple of extra minutes during the first class and at the end of the last class, but it was worth it.

How would you set up your room to maximize your teaching style?

We have already discussed the expectations you have to set up in your class based on behaviors.

We went over how you should deliver your instruction and your content.

Now it is time to investigate how your classroom should look.

II.
How your seats are set up is important.

You can set up desks in rows, which works for a lot of teachers. I have seen some great teachers who have their desks in rows.

I know a lot of people who think rows are antiquated and promote a lecture-based classroom. Lancaster required rows; that's enough for me to not use them.

However, I have seen it work in many classrooms and works well for testing situations. I know most humanities classes regard this as horrible, but I have seen it work in those classes as well. It is more about the teacher, really.

Students facing each other with a space for you to walk down the middle allows for debates and discussions. All the students can pretty much see each other and it promotes a more interactive environment.

Small three or four desk clusters could also be a great option. It allows for group collaboration. The drawbacks are group discussions and testing.

The horseshoe or U-shape is what most humanities teachers like. It allows students to see each other and again allows for a more interactive class. However, it is difficult for testing situations and you have a good amount of empty space.

How you set the seats up should enhance the way you want to teach your class. No one way is right or wrong, it just depends on your style.

When it comes to seat arrangement you should explore multiple formats and arrangements until the one you like emerges.

Keep trying new things. This is one of those things you have to try out to see if it works every year or break. You can change it multiple times a year just to keep it fresh.

Classroom size is also factor of how you can set up your room. Physical space can help or hinder.

For years I used the horseshoe shape. It allowed me to engage with the class and fostered the most amount of discussion.

However, for testing, I would make each student move their desk into the open spaces. It looked like the desks exploded around the room. All the physical floor space should be taken up and nobody was seated next to another person. They could even turn their desks to face different directions. They all liked this because it promoted a positive testing environment where nobody could see another's paper.

Side note concerning testing: I would also tell them if I saw anyone looking around the room or what looked like cheating I would just write their name on a piece of paper. I wouldn't call them out or engage with them during the test. I would just give them a zero and tell them after class. It's very effective.

Currently, in my search for a different work environment, I eschewed desks and moved to tables. Now, students sit at tables set up in a large U-shape. They sit on the inside and outside of the tables.

It has promoted a different level of discussion and collaboration because the tables can be moved and situated differently. I am also in one of the biggest rooms in my school. I am here by design. My principal has allowed me to experiment with this new class to see if it changes student interaction and collaboration. I love it.

III.

The next consideration you have is where the students sit. You have two choices here: Have a seating chart or don't.

Seating charts allow for you to remember names faster. It helps a great deal in the first two weeks.

I don't have a seating chart. I like to let students choose where they sit on a daily basis. It makes me have to play a "name game" the first week of school to get to know students. This is also a game where we build community and the other students learn their classmates' names.

I like giving the students a choice of where they can sit. It allows them some autonomy.

Sometimes I have to move students because they get too distracted.

Other times I move the entire class to give kids a new perspective on the class. I tell the whole class to move to another seat in the room, where they cannot sit next to anyone they have previously sat next to. I do this a couple of times a year. It changes up the environment and their perspective, allowing them to interact with different students and not just their friends.

No matter what our desk set up looks like or how you seat your students, the goal is to maintain a learning environment that leads to student achievement in your classroom.

Use what you want, how you want. Experiment and don't let anyone else dictate how students learn in your class.

When I was a novice teacher and trying a bunch of ideas, I had kids sitting on the floor, on low, waist-high bookshelves, I even had one kid who sat on top of a filing cabinet.

My philosophy is simple. Sit where you want (except in my chair, behind my desk) as long as you are learning and not a distraction.

By the way, I keep my desk in full view of the door for safety reasons and because we have windows in the door and I can see if anyone is looking in. Or otherwise.

IV.

The walls are a different story.

Whatever you do please, please, please don't put up stupid motivational posters!

If you do, I just might come by and graffiti them in the middle of the night.

Why would you waste the time and money?

Why would you visually assault your students with that crap?

Why would you want a picture of some kitten hanging off a tree branch with "Hang in there" written in the corner... ugghh!

I want a poster that just shows an empty tree branch with claw marks that says "Bye! Try again tomorrow"

That would be cool.

You should take pride in your room and put up wall art that first and foremost interests you. Then it should be something that makes students think.

I have movie posters from some of my favorite books and movies in my room. I have always had *The Breakfast Club* movie poster and the *Animal House* John Belushi "College" sweatshirt portrait on my wall. They go with me to every room I've had.

The rest have changed over the years.

I also have a wall behind my desk where I put pictures, posters, art, and magnets that I like. I have everything from a poster of my favorite band from one of their tours to interesting sayings on magnets.

I have an Edgar Allen Poe action figure still in the box that a student got me years ago that I hang on the wall. I have a "Don't Panic" poster from *The Hitchhiker's Guide to the Galaxy*. I have a sign that says "No Whining" and a plaque from "The National Sarcasm Society."

And of course I have pictures of my family.

The point is, I have things that make me feel good and that I want to look at. Some are gifts from students and other things I buy specifically for the wall. Students like looking at them and asking questions about the stuff. It engages them.

I also have collected a good amount of student artwork over the years. The best ones I keep on my wall. I have a pencil drawn portrait of me a student did for art class and a portrait of Shakespeare done where the words to *Romeo and Juliet* that makes up the picture. I have a few paintings that students have done: one says "Rebel", another says, "No Matter, Try Again, Fail Again, Fail Better," and another that says, "May the Force be with you."

My favorite is the word "Create" done with nails hammered into a board and different colored string wrapped between the nails that actually "create" the word. It was given to me by the mother of a student who passed away a few years ago, and it is very special to me.

Let's talk bulletin boards.

I have always had two huge bulletin boards in my class that I had to fill. I got an idea years ago from a colleague to fill the boards with articles and pictures cut out from magazines I get throughout the year.

Every month I get a lot of magazines. Any picture or article that I think is interesting I put on the board. Actors, athletes, musicians, cool advertisements, one-page stories and interviews, cool graphics and sometimes, just images I like. It ranges from Entrepreneur magazine and Fast Company to Rolling Stone, Esquire, and GQ. I use Time magazine and The Washington Post as well. Pretty much anything is fair game. When I started teaching, I collected old magazines from friends, family and the school library.

I cut out the pictures and articles and save them so I can change the board every year. The students love the boards because we can engage in discussions about what they see up there. I suggest you do this as it is engaging and interesting for the students. It is a conversation starter.

V.

The point of a good classroom set up is engagement. Is your class set up to foster the type of thinking, discussion, practice that you want from your students?

Is your classroom a place that you want to walk into and be a part of for the entire day?

Is it inviting and comfortable?

Is it interesting and functional for the discipline you teach?

Is everything you need, or students need, accessible before, during, or after class?

You want to minimize distractions when students come in late or during class.

I think of a classroom as an extension of my home. It combines form and function.

I have my kitchen set up a specific way so that it I feel good when I walk into it to cook. It is also set up to allow for the most functional use of space. I don't have the things I use on a daily basis — knives, cutting boards, salt — far away from each other. I have them grouped to allow for the best process for how I work.

The same is true for your classroom. It should be inviting and functional, as well as safe.

I find that a lot of teachers just have space they take up for teaching, but it isn't a reflection of who they really are.

You might think it isn't important, and I would agree to some degree.

College classes are universal and not personal.

In some countries, like Japan, the teachers move from class to class, and the students are static. But the classrooms I saw had the students' personalities represented on the walls. It was like the students took responsibility for the space and made it their own.

If you are a minimalist, then go with that. If you love stuff everywhere, then go with that.

Your classroom should be an extension of who you are and how you want your students to react to how and what you teach.

Make the space yours as much as you can.

But for everyone's sake, do not put up silly motivational posters!

Unless you need to motivate yourself; in that case, you should give up now.

Chapter Nine

The Professional

I.
Learning to teach is only one side of the coin. The other side is the professional life.

How do you want to be seen as a teacher?

Let's start with the beginning.

Most teachers HATE the first week school. The reason is simple. The first week is not spent doing what you signed up for - TEACHING. You are not really getting your classroom ready for the new year either. That comes last. You are attending to all the other stuff you have to do. Most of that stuff has nothing to do with teaching, you or your kids, but is SO important to the "higher-ups."

It's all about meetings, meetings, meetings where people drone on and on about new initiatives, software, data collection, assessments, teacher evaluations, etc… blah, blah, blah.

Most of the time, these new initiatives aren't fully fleshed out and it feels like we are always "building the plane while flying it." I love this idea!

It happens year after year. It never fails to make me shake my head and smile.

We teachers are expected to learn all the new stuff and incorporate it all right away. Be ready. Every year, there will be new stuff coming at you.

It could be getting new textbooks or new curriculum guides with school wide trainings that are supposed to change everything we do as teachers "for the better."

It could be new administrators or principals coming in with new ideas and telling you how things are going to work from here on in.

It could be new technology. The learning curve on new technology, both hardware and software can also make life more difficult when you are trying to get ready for the new year.

The frustrations are many.

Sometimes the technology comes in the day before students arrive or the login screens don't accept the passwords because of a firewall or something else to make you scream ARRGGHH!

The bottom line is that every "first week" for teachers is always one thing or another, a seemingly endless amount of information and tasks that you somehow have to become an "expert" in right now or the school year can't start properly.

Then some, most, or all of it changes the next year!
You start two steps behind.
So what do you do?
How should you handle all this?

You smile, nod, and roll with it.

Why?

You are a professional.

You meet the deadlines, you fill out the forms, you watch the training videos, and you set your goals - trying to make them as meaningful as possible.

You collect the data, you learn the technology, and you read the articles; you do what has to be done.

You try starting only one step behind.

You don't spend hours whining and complaining about it.

You grit your teeth and get it done as soon as possible.

You are a professional.

Because for every minute that you are pushing back against the machine or refusing to submit out of righteous indignation, you are spending time away from what really matters...

Getting your classroom ready and preparing for your students.

That is why you are here.

With that being said, sometimes protest is necessary. The point is to know the difference. Watch some of the veterans you admire.

Pick your battles.

You should register a complaint when warranted or be angry about some new initiative that you know is stupid. A lot of them are.

You should fire off an email to your union building rep or to the principal if you need to. You should become part of a Faculty Advisory Committee in order to file complaints and be heard through union channels.

If your voice isn't being heard find ways in which it can be. Use them.

You should write scathing commentaries and op-ed pieces and try to get them published in the local paper or even bigger. If that is what you feel like you should do.

Write away... blog away... comment away. But don't just complain about the profession. (Note: Careful what you put on the Internet. People have been fired for posting negative articles, blogs, and comments on social media.)

But remember, if it is more important for you to "rage against the institution" than it is to focus on your students, and on yourself in being the best teacher you can, then what are you really doing?

If you can do both... GREAT!

Most can't and the latter suffers. Don't lose your perspective and don't forget the big picture. Don't let your eyes leave the prize.

Choose your battles. Choose them wisely.

Make sure your students come BEFORE your personal issues/gripes/anger.

Leave the garbage out of the classroom. When you walk in your classroom with your students, the "teacher you" is on.

Remember why you are there.
You are a professional.
You are a teacher.

II.

Both students and colleagues notice your daily conduct at school. What you do and what you say. How you act and how you react.

How do you want people to "see you"?

It all adds up to your professionalism as an educator.

It establishes your credibility.

You have to think about what you want now and in the future.

I made a decision a long time ago to always be smiling when I enter my building.

First, I believe I have an incredible job and I can't believe I get to do it. I love what I do and it makes me happy every day. It doesn't mean I don't have bad days or come into the building feeling poorly on some days, I just try not to show it.

Second, I make sure that in my interactions with colleagues and students that I portray myself as feeling good and looking forward to each day.

It is a mindset that has served me well over the years.

Feeling good, being excited about the day, and believing that I "get to" not "have to" teach makes a difference.

If people see you as a positive, proactive and good teacher who puts their students first (even if that means upsetting the apple cart at times), treats others politely and with respect, and is consistently looking to better the practice, don't you think doors will open for you and bigger opportunities will come to you?

Do you think the "negative" teachers get the option to teach specialized programs like AP or IB? Do you think they get chosen for leadership roles in their building?

Don't think that being professional is simply about minding your p's and q's. It's not. Speak up. If you feel strongly on an issue, say so.

You can do it professionally. And you can do it as problem solver, not a problem.

I have a colleague who is very outspoken about everything. She is also one of the best teachers in the building. The principal, whom she is often at odds with, nominated her for Teacher of the Year one year.

To be blunt, it's simple: don't be a jackass.

Put your students and your practice first, and then make observations and criticisms. Then you will be seen as an asset, as somebody people want to work with.

What do you think the teacher who constantly complains or is a complete downer and treats colleagues poorly is going to get?

Do you think anyone is going to offer that person anything to advance their careers?

Not likely.

Are you a positive and proactive professional in your building and within your community? Think about it.

How do people really see you?

Look around your building. What type of people receive new opportunities to be heard, to move into leadership roles, to get the first chance to teach new and exciting programs, or to be involved with others at a deeper level?

The professionals.

What are the others getting?

They are the ones usually complaining they didn't get the opportunity that the others got.

I wonder why?

While we are on the subject- how do you deal with those individuals, your colleagues, who constantly complain? Especially when they are your friends.

I try to disassociate myself with them over time. I try not to engage with them. If I have to, I let it go in one ear and out the next. I don't try to change their minds; some people like to complain and feel it is their duty to do so. Whatever.

I try to remember, although it is hard to do, that I can't always change my situation, but I can change my reaction to it.

Try not to let the vampires suck the life out of you with their negativity. Let it be their issue not yours.

III.

Afterschool clubs, activities, and sports are vital to the school community. They need you.

If you have a particular sport you are qualified to coach or help out with, it is good to get involved.

Maybe you sponsor a club that the students put together. It can be a service club, a religious club, a national club, or even a fun club.

Either way, it is good to see students outside the classroom. They need us to sponsor these activities, and we need to support them. It is also good that they see us in a less academic environment.

Extracurricular involvement is part of being a professional.

Just don't do any your first year of teaching. You have too much on your plate. Some administrators "prey" upon the new teachers to help them fill voids in the coaching or sponsoring roles. Say no your first year. Then decide.

I have been the golf coach every year since my second year of teaching and I have sponsored the same club for fourteen years, every Wednesday after school. It is rewarding, and in most places you get paid for sports. Bonus!

IV.

How you develop professionally is vital to crafting yourself as a professional teacher.

The opportunities that you seek outside of the classroom build you into a better teacher.

Look for opportunities to learn new skills, content knowledge -- any way to develop professionally.

Get your Master's degree.

Go to an Advanced Placement Summer Institute.

Then put in an application to be an AP reader.

Learn new technology and actually use it.
Get Nationally Board Certified.
Become a mentor teacher.
Learn about global education.
Attend professional conferences.
Become a part of a policy group.

Do anything that helps you learn more. It advances your career and it models for your students that you are a life-long learner.

Professional development is just that.

But it is not just regulated to your professional practice.

Developing new hobbies or furthering your current hobbies will help your practice.

I have a colleague who recently took up photography. He is so excited about learning his new craft that he talks about it all the time. He has inspired some of his students to take it up as well. They talk all the time now before and after school, they show each other their work and they critique it. It has been a great learning experience for all involved.

At the top of my list is travel. I can't stress enough how important it is. It widens your perspective, challenges your beliefs, and creates understanding. Your development as a global citizen inspires others.

Your traveling stories are also great for the classroom. The travel can be local, state, national, or international.

Travel can be by yourself, with your friends, family, colleagues or even with a tour company like EF where you travel with your students.

It doesn't really matter. Just go.

Then tell your students the stories.

Talk with and to your students about your interests. You will develop a connection with them, and it benefits both of you.

IV.

You have, we all have, beliefs about people, society, and the world.

We also have what Atticus Finch calls "blind spots."

Everyone has them.

You have to look at yourself and identify yours. You should know and understand what you believe about people and the world.

Your beliefs about race, culture, poverty, religions, political parties, and your stereotypes about people can influence your teaching in a negative way.

Then, before you enter your classroom you have to check any and all limiting bias you have at the door. It has to stay outside of the room.

This is not an easy task, but it has to be done. It is nearly impossible to be completely unbiased, but acknowledging it and actively working against it is imperative.

Take all the things you believe that could hinder your belief that all students have the right, ability, and capacity to learn, and leave them outside of the classroom.

When your students walk into your room, they are not to be walking into a biased environment.

Why? Because your job isn't to pass your beliefs and/or stereotypes, negative or not, on to your students, or hinder in any way, shape or form your students' learning.

Engage and explore your beliefs, and ask yourself if you can see another perspective. This will help you and your students.

Think about the model minority myth about Asians. Do you believe it?

What about myths concerning other minorities, or marginalized groups? Do you believe them?

What consequence do you think these beliefs could have in your classroom?

If you are religious and believe your religion is "the right one" and that others are "not right," then what influence might that have on your students?

Your job is to teach and let them make decisions about what they believe on their own. It isn't your job to teach them what you think is right.

Let's be real.

I understand that some beliefs we hold deeply seem almost impossible to check at the door. You are not discarding what you believe.

You simply are keeping it yourself if it somehow marginalizes students or makes them feel uncomfortable in your room. That will interfere with their learning.

You don't come first. Your students do when they are in your classroom.

If you don't believe in abortion or have an opinion that homosexuality is wrong, don't bring it into the classroom.

Politics, religion, race, how poverty affects generations, drug abuse, war, etc., your opinions, your beliefs are not what you are hired to teach.

You need to remain neutral.

Two things my students do not know about me: My religion or my political beliefs. They ask, and ask often, but I will not tell them.

I once had a particularly savvy student ask me about being married. He mentioned that if I was married then it was probably in a church and most likely by a priest or a minister. Therefore, I must be a Christian of some sort. Great logic. I applauded the student while the rest sat on the edges of their seat waiting for an answer.

My reply: Yes, I am married. Yes, a minister married me, but he was a life-long friend of my wife's and her family. It was non-negotiable that he married us. But, a marriage is both a religious and a state contract that is conducted by a person who has the credentials to do so. Any religion that was infused into the ceremony was for my wife and her family. That is not to say I didn't believe in it but it was for my wife, not necessarily for me. That is a part of being together. The give and take of things that is important to individuals. And we were married outside under a canopy of trees on the bank of a river. Not a church in sight.

My personal and political beliefs do not come into play into my classroom. When I am judging a debate my students are having concerning gun control in America, the side that presents the best argument is the one that will win the debate. Not the one that I believe is correct based on what I believe.

Check your bias at the door. It is vital.

Your job is to create a safe learning environment where everyone has a voice and feels comfortable learning in your room.

You are a professional.

V.

A good practitioner must reflect on their practice.

This is not easy.

When you are student teaching, you have multiple eyes on you at any given time. The mentor teacher, the supervisor of your student teaching experience, and any other number of stakeholders in your student teaching experience observe you. You are given daily, weekly, monthly feedback both verbally and written. This is a huge benefit.

However, when you actually get your own classroom, you are left on your own to "see" your practice and improve upon it. Sure, you have the annual or semi-annual evaluation by somebody in the building. That is the basic "this teacher is competent" evaluation but doesn't contain any real constructive or meaningful feedback for reflective introspection.

These reviews are often cloudy and don't give what you really need to improve your professional practice.

Teachers prepare for these evaluations with some perfect lesson plan that we devised for just that day. The 'dog and pony' show to make sure we pass. It isn't real.

But what about the other days of the school year? What about the hours, days, weeks, months where we are alone in our rooms and teach by ourselves? How do you evaluate those?

You need to be able to do this yourself.

Here are a few questions you can ask to reflect on your practice:

> Was what I did today successful? How do I know?
> What formative or summative assessment shows this?
> What went well today? Why?
> What didn't go well today? Why?
> How was my "management" of class? What could I do better?
> How was my delivery? How can I gauge what I said was understood?
> Did I teach or reinforce the necessary skills?
> Was my content good?
> Was I engaging? How do I know?
> Where are my strengths?
> What are my weaknesses?
> How can I improve what I am doing?
> What do I need to do tomorrow?

You have to be honest with yourself, the good and the bad.

Give yourself a pat on the back for the good and then address the bad.

Get yourself a journal or create a file on your computer and use these questions as a guide for reflecting on what you are doing. Do this daily or weekly.

You have to be honest with yourself and your practice.

You could also do this by asking a colleague to come into your room to evaluate you. Ask someone you trust, whom you think is a good teacher and will give you open and honest feedback.

You can record your classroom. Get a camera stand for your phone and set it up on your desk. Record a warm up or a lesson, and review it for yourself. Watch what you are doing and ask yourself how you can improve. If you don't know how to fix something, then ask a colleague you trust and think is a good teacher.

You could also ask your students to fill out a survey that you create. That is a wake up call.

I have an end-of-year student evaluation I give out after the final, like in college, that makes me take a hard look at some of the things I do that students don't like. It's hard...but worth it. (Make sure you listen to the good things students say as well! We often focus too much on the bad things.)

One of the hardest parts of becoming a Nationally Board Certified Teacher is the reflective piece. You have to confront both what you do well and what you don't do well. Another "blind spot."

Once you start to see these, you can build your practice proactively and improve.

This is crafting your practice.

This is being a teacher.

VI.

When it comes to your professional life as a teacher, you must also adhere to a few other duties.

Messing up any of these on a consistent basis is a way for administration to give you more attention than you really want to have.

It is not being professional.

These are things that can enhance or hinder your career. They aren't tough to follow if you get into the routine of doing them

You have to keep accurate records. Keeping a detailed account of attendance is very important. You need to know who was in your class on what day. If they weren't in class, you need to know why. Are you seeing a trend in absences? This could be indicative of larger problems. Are they absent from your class and not others?

Students get sick, students skip class; these things happen. You can't get to the bottom of a situation, help another teacher, the administration, or parents get answers if you don't know if a student is chronically sick, or just skipping a single class.

You can't help if you don't know. So know. Pay attention.

You have to talk to other teachers, parents, and/or administration to see what is going on with certain students. This is imperative.

Do it.

You need to keep an accurate and up-to-date grade book. Period.

Your grade book must also be transparent to students, parents, and administration. This could mean the difference between a student graduating or not.

Maintaining an accurate and transparent grade book also helps you with any issue you might have with a parent or student complaining about a grade. Grades should create a clear dialogue with all stakeholders involved.

Some teachers wait until the very last minute before putting grades in their grade book. Grades on an assignment, or the lack of a grade due to a missing assignment, should not be a surprise to the student or parent. Your grades should be updated in a timely fashion before the grading period is over.

If you don't do this, you may run into a problem with an administrator changing a grade to please a parent. This happens.

If your grades are kept up-to-date and transparent, then the ownership and responsibility of those grades falls directly on the student's shoulders.

If a student fails the class, the student fails. If you fail the student, you fail.

Keep up with technology. You don't have to use it. But you should know a bit about it.

Most studies show that adding and incorporating more and more technology doesn't improve student learning.

American classrooms have more tech than any other country and it hasn't helped improve test scores.

However, it is the way of the world these days and can be very useful.

If you are extremely tech savvy then use it if you can justify how it helps students.

If not, don't over reach. Don't use it just to use it. But don't be afraid of learning something new that can be useful in the classroom.

Communicating with families is also important. You don't have to wait to have a conference with a parent in order to talk with them. I know a colleague who calls each student's parents the first week of school. Daunting, but it works for him.

Maybe you will decide to take five minutes to call parents to tell them how great a particular student was in class that day. That karma pays, especially if it is a struggling student.

Technology can also help with communication. Use it any way you can to foster that relationship with the family. Collect email addresses in the beginning of the year and email parents. Let them know the great things that are happening or the concerns you have.

No matter what the situation, when you communicate with parents I have two standard rules.

Never meet with a parent alone. Too much can go wrong. It can become a "he said-she said" environment, which can never be good. Always have another teacher, department chair, counselor, or administrator in the room.

When it comes to conferences, always start the conversation with a parent about their student with a positive comment, no matter what!

I don't care if that student is the bane of your existence, find something good to say.

There has to be something good about the student's behavior or work that you can come up with. If not, make something up. Maybe you comment that they always show up on time, or the student is really quite funny at times. Don't lead the conference conversation with the student's disruptive behavior or how the student is a spiteful little troublemaker.

Parents coming in for conferences are often ready for battle with the teachers. This usually isn't their first time in the conference arena. They have an agenda and often the student (for self-preservation purposes) has pitted the two factions against each other. Fault and blame are nebulous things.

If the student is having trouble in your room, then chances are they are having trouble in all their classes.

Imagine being a parent and having five to seven teachers, a counselor, and maybe an administrator ready to jump on them and tell them how "bad" their student is in school. This isn't a positive environment for all those involved. It can be antagonistic and can get ugly quick.

I have seen some parents escorted out by security and banned from school grounds. It's true and it happens.

Be clear with your concerns about behavior, attendance, the student's grades, and be proactive with how you want to work together in order to help the student achieve in your class.

Conferences should be solutions-based. They should be based on what should happen in the future, not dwelling on what has happened in the past.

Start with telling parents something positive, then move to the concern, then move to the solution. "How can we do X to benefit the student?"

It works. It is less antagonistic and usually relieves the pressure. It creates clear lines of communication between you and the parent. You both have the same goal— to help the student achieve.

VII.
Appearance matters.

Clothes speak volumes.

How you are dressed in school informs others how you want to be seen.

Sometimes your school has a dress code. If so, follow it. If not, then determine your own. This goes back to how you want the world to see you.

The concept of dressing professionally is a slippery slope. The definition of "professional attire" is very open-ended.

We live in a new world of casual. But just because we are more casual, it doesn't mean it has to equal sloppy. Sloppy is sad.

Should you wear a suit or a shirt and tie to school every day if you are male? Should you wear a pantsuit or a dress to school every day if you are female?

You decide.

Whatever you do, make sure you look good for you. You should be neat, clean, have clothes that fit, and you should be covered.

You should be yourself. Be authentic to who you are. Your clothes should represent you and how you want to be seen.

I have a colleague who wears a shirt and tie every day. It works for him. I have another colleague who wears a skirt/dress every day. It works for her.

I do not wear a tie, nor do I wear a skirt.

I wear a collared shirt tucked in, or a sweater. I wear chinos or jeans. I wear nice shoes, never sneakers, and I shave every day. My clothes are clean, they fit and I never look like a student. This is my standard. I wear the same thing outside of school for the most part.

I have always had a problem with the word "professionally dressed" when I have seen men wearing pants that are too long, ill-fitting shirts, ties that are too long and scuffed shoes. This to me is not professional.

Women, you may have different standards, however, clothing guidelines should fall under the clean and well-fitting aspect. And of course, your clothing should cover the places you don't want students to see. You know what I mean.

Tattoos? Piercings? Up to you, or up to your school.

Dress the way you want to be seen.

Dress authentically.

Dress how you see yourself as a teacher

VIII.

Being professional means different things to different people.

However, there are lines, some are blurry, some are absolutely not! You know what I mean.

Here are some of my "rules" for professionalism.

I do not follow or accept friend requests on social media until after graduation.

I do not touch, other than the occasional handshake, high five or fist bump. Hugs are for very special occasions like winning an award or getting into college, but mainly only at graduation and only if the student requests one.

Never be in a room alone with a student. Period. One teacher and one student in a room is a recipe for disaster.

If you need to talk to a student alone try to go into the hallway.

People talk... kids talk...Parents talk. What do you want your reputation to be?

Also, it is important that you engage and interact with everyone in the building, not just other teachers.

All custodian staff — you should know their names.

All the support staff, the same.

Don't forget, these people are really the ones that run the school on a day-to-day basis. Treat them kindly and understand that you all work together and nobody works beneath you. A school is a community.

Keep a clear head in faculty and department meetings. Unhappy teachers tend to complain a great deal and want to be the center of attention. Listen to them at the time and decide if it's important. If it's not, throw it out. Don't buy into their issues. Keep quiet. If it involves you and affects you, then focus on how to solve the problem.

Faculty meetings can and are often boring and you can feel that they are a waste of time. You should bring something to grade.

When you treat yourself and others as professionals then others will treat you as one as well.

As Steven Pressfield says in his book Turning Pro, "Be a pro."

Be a teacher.

Chapter Ten

The [R]Evolution

I.
It is time.

Time to rise above and resist.

Rise above and resist the status quo.

Rise above and resist what they think a good teacher looks like.

Rise above and resist the garbage they feed you about what student achievement looks like.

The revolution is slowly unfolding across the nation. Teachers, students, parents, and education stakeholders have started the shift.

The institutions are not going to change until we change them.

AND...

It is time for a change.

It is time to redefine what we need in our schools.

This isn't about policy at the school, district, or state level.

We have heard this call for years. We need schools modeled after Finland, Singapore, Korea, etc.

These aren't perfect school systems- they are pretty much homogenous and smaller than us here in the States, but it's a start.

We need to model our schools to look like the top PISA scoring schools in the world if we are going to compete in a global economy.

We need to re-imagine and re-invigorate the students and the teachers in our schools.

The issue is that most of these "calls to action" are student focused. They talk about how we need to change the way we do things to help our students achieve in the 21st century.

I totally agree, but part of the issue is that they don't talk about how to improve the teachers and the profession who is going to help these students.

We live in a country where teachers have been vilified.

We need a system that re-imagines, re-invigorates, re-inspires, and re-ignites how we train and mentor teachers to actually effect the change that is needed.

II.
We must evolve and realize that learning to be a teacher is as important as learning to teach. We need to be clear on the ways in which we think about teaching, both in the classroom and outside.

We need to understand and value the craft.

We need more information, more support, more mentors, more innovation, more freedom, and more of the unmitigated belief that our students really come first.

We need to work together collaboratively not competitively.

We need the [Re]education of teachers and a [R]evolution in the way we train them.

We need paradigm shift in what it means to be a teacher in this country.

We expect our teachers to teach our students to become globally minded, innovative and entrepreneurial, yet we are still training these teachers in the same way we did ten, twenty, fifty, even one-hundred years ago; it doesn't make sense.

We can't train teachers the same way and expect them to train our students in another. I think there is something about the definition of insanity here.

Things need to shift, to equalize, and the expectations need to change.

This isn't going happen in a one-day professional development workshop where most teachers have tuned out and are grading papers.

Is isn't going to happen until we model those cutting edge schools and teacher training schools of education across the nation until they become the norm.

But how do we shift right now?

How do we actually make this change?

It is time for you to take what you learned in school, what you learned during your internship, and/or during your first years of teaching and decide what is useful and what isn't, what hinders you and what helps.

Use the fire and burn whatever you don't need.

Move forward and evolve.

III.

Recently, we have seen a massive change in the world in how we do business in this new global economy.

Schools over the last 100 years prepared students for the 20th century world in which they lived.

However, that world is no more.

The manufacturing that helped create the middle class in America is pretty much gone, and we have ushered in the brave new world of the Internet and technology.

But, where are the jobs?

The world isn't changing; it has already changed.

And jobs focusing on technology, science, teaching, and/or jobs that focus on customer service are growing.

But the real future of American business is the same as it was 100 years ago, Entrepreneurship.

Creating a system that promotes entrepreneurship in our students is what we need to be doing.

We have been preparing our students for the results of the Industrial Revolution 100 years ago. Those manufacturing jobs present in the 20th century are all but gone today.

Now we need to create students that are prepared for the world in the 21st century and maybe even the 22nd century.

Now we need to look toward the future and ask ourselves: Are we really preparing our students for the world in which they live? (watch the *Shift Happens* videos on YouTube.)

Are we creating students with the ability and spirit to lead us into the future the way they did 100 years ago?

This country made huge economic, scientific and cultural advances due to the abilities and entrepreneurship of its people.

Are we honoring the past, the present, and preparing for the future?

The short answer is no.

But the answer is not as simple as that…

Some have already taken this challenge and small pockets of change are rising up and going against the institutions that perpetuate the status quo.

Montessori schools, High Tech High schools, AP Capstone and IB programs, Khan Academy, and the Un-schooling and home schooling movement are just to name a few on a long list. And, yes, I know these systems aren't perfect either, but they are a step in the right direction. Google them.

Tony Wagner's books, *The Global Achievement Gap*, *Creating Innovators* and *Most Likely to Succeed* should be required reading for every teacher in the country.

Look into The Asia Society, Teachers for Global Classrooms (IREX), the Fulbright programs and The World Affairs Council that support global education. (See Resource page)

Investigate, explore, read, and use their ideas and resources … over and over.

IV.

The role of the 21st century teacher has to be two-fold. The same ideas should be used for both students and teachers. We should be teaching teachers these skills!

You can have an impact on students when you talk about, and model for them, how you fulfill these for yourself.

We need teachers and students to:

> Develop a sense of inquiry about the world.
> Encourage and be motivated to reach their goals.
> Listen to others and offer constructive advice.
> Analyze and synthesize information effectively.
> Learn and practice how to argue.

Reflect on their learning and the world.
Look for leadership opportunities.
Discover how to access information in new ways.
Create a space for exploring the world.

It is time to decide how you will:

Disrupt the status quo.
Think divergently.
Go against the grain.
Swim against the stream.
Be different.

This is where I tell you to think outside the box, however, the problem with that is most people don't know what box they are in.

Thinking outside the box is garbage.

You can't think outside the box if you don't know what box you're in!

What box were you placed in by your education, your college, and/or your current school?

What limits and constrictions have they placed on you? What have they stifled in you?

What have they told you that you can't do? Shouldn't do?

What restrictions have you placed on yourself due to your beliefs?

What have you told yourself you can't do because its not 'the way things are done'?

What kind of teacher do you really want to be?

THINK, REFLECT, DEFINE, AND DECIDE. BECOME.

V.

What is more important: inspiring students or making them compete against each other?

A lot of daily school is the illusion of education.

How many students look forward to coming to class where they know they are going to be graded on things they don't really care about OR they look forward to being graded because they have memorized every word.

In a system where a student's self-esteem is tied to grades, we have created a space where a teacher can control too much.

One bad teacher or a handful of bad grades can do a lot of damage to a student's self-esteem and self-worth.

Or the student learns to navigate the system by being "The perfect student" — studying (memorizing) and playing nice.

They get the good grades, the great self-esteem, but when they get to college, or go into the world, they are woefully unprepared.

What does that do to them?

Grades are really part of the illusion. They create a system of competition where students don't place value on what they are learning but rather what grade they will get.

Ask them about it. I've talked to hundreds of students about this and they mostly agree: it's all about the grades!

Students have value and gifts that can never be quantified with grades in a classroom. When they are put under this system, it diminishes their capacity to achieve, it doesn't encourage it; it actually crushes it.

Yes, you have to give grades to students in this day and age. But when you tell them that the grade isn't the most important thing in your class and that what they are learning is way more important, you can feel them change and grow.

When you tell them you want to see them try and fail, but fail better next time (Samuel Beckett) and that you will assess them on that…

Wow… do things change.

Check out Alfie Kohn's work on abolishing grades and the idea of competition in schools; it changes things.

VI.

Think about what you want to teach, what grades, what levels within those grades. What special programs: AP, IB, ESOL, etc.

Good teachers know why they are teaching and why they should teach the classes they teach.

Simon Sinek's brilliant TED Talk raises our understanding of "why."

He explains how we usually move from "what" to "how" to "why."

The "what" is what we are doing (teaching) to the "how" (delivering instruction) and the "why" (because we want students to learn).

What we should be doing is moving in the opposite direction. We should start with the "why" then move to the "how" and then the "what."

He states: "People don't buy what you do; they buy why you do it."

If you are passionate about helping students and they know "why" you do it, then how you deliver instruction becomes easier, then what you are doing is seen as a positive interaction. Student achievement happens.

How many students could achieve more if they understood the "why" in what you are doing?

Or even better, the "why" of what they are doing.

Too many students that I have spoken with don't understand "why" they are really in school taking a bunch of classes. They know the "how"-- by sitting in multiple classes a day and memorizing the information. They know the "what"-- to get into college and get a good job.

What if students really understood the "why" of being in school?

What if they could "buy" into what they are doing because they actually see the connection to their future?

It would be a game-changer, for all stakeholders.

Back to you…

We talked about your "why" in the first chapter. Did you ever answer that question?

Remember the fire?

It is time to seek out those on the cutting edge of pedagogy; the teachers, authors, administrators, schools, and organizations who are challenging the status quo and trying to re-stamp school.

Find them online, on social media, in articles and feature stories-

It is up to you to read, watch, experiment, with new ideas in your classroom.

It is time to investigate programs for your education or your school that allow you to join the ranks of others turning their backs on the old system.

Remember Gandhi's quote: "Be the change you wish to see in the world."

It's to join the [R]Evolution of education.

You are part of the fire that will keep this going.

You are a teacher in the 21st century.

Chapter Eleven

The Teacher

I.
You need to be the teacher you would want to learn from.

You have to inspire and be inspired.

What inspires you? Why?

You need to be honest about who you are and what you can and can't do.

How well do you know your subject? How good of a classroom "manager" are you?

How do you deliver your content? How do you talk to your students?

How do you ask for help? Whom would you ask for help?

How are your students experiencing what you are doing?

Remember the old saying: Students will not remember what you taught them, but how you made them feel.

When you are able to reflect on these ideas and have solid answers, you are becoming a teacher.

Are you excited?

II.

Remember the "why" question?

Little children ask this question often. If you have a child or have been around little kids then you know all too well how often this is asked.

How do you answer?

Most of the time the answer from an authority figure is "because" or "because I said so."

Most children stop asking because they don't get the answers they want or they were told again and again to stop asking so many questions.

This also happens in school classrooms; students are told to stop asking and just listen for the answers. No need to question, the teacher is the source of all the knowledge they will need.

When my son was four, he asked "why" over and over and over. I often answered him and then he would follow it up with "why" again, and we would head down the rabbit hole of "why, why, why?"! ARRGGHH!

It was frustrating because he wasn't satisfied with the answer because he didn't understand the answer I gave him. It's not really his fault, because he is searching for understanding.

Then I read a book that my wife gave me that suggested I reply to him by asking him the question, "Why do you think?"

It's a world of difference.

He would answer and funny enough most of the time the answer didn't make sense, but he was working through it.

That was way better than me just telling him.

Now increase his age and experience.

What could happen if we develop his own interests by asking him that question and giving him the tools (talking it out with me, or working on a computer) where he could access answers and possibly more understanding?

That would be interesting.

What if we grew a whole new generation of students (and teachers) that asked "why" and needed to know the answers before moving on?

We could change education.

III.

Let's look at this in a practical sense.

As teachers, we are taught, and it can be a good idea for your first couple of years, to maintain "control over the class."

What I mean is that you have to be able to direct the class where you want to go and make sure everything is being steered the way you want it.

The feeling you have when you lose control of a class is horrible; it can actually be frightening.

It is a feeling you never forget nor want to relive.

Don't worry about it and don't be afraid of it; it will happen. Ride the wave and reflect on what happened, how you felt, what went wrong, and how can you use what you learned so it doesn't happen again.

But it will happen, probably more than once and for different reasons.

It's okay. Learn from it.

Eventually, you will move into a "quiet command" of the class. That is where your classroom "management," your personality, your reputation with students, and your inherent authority and experience will all coalesce and class will seem to run itself with minimal effort on your part.

If you are able, take a personal day or ask your principal for a professional day and find a master teacher in your building.

Watch their Zen-like control of the classroom, their expectations being met, their delivery of content, and the whole thing.

Then ask them how they do it! (Sometimes they can't exactly articulate it; they just do it. Watch them closely and see if you can pick up on what it is they are doing.)

Then take it back to your classroom and model it.

Customize it for your classes.

Once you have 'the presence' and can replicate it in other classes, push yourself a little more.

Go for controlled chaos.

Controlled chaos can be fun! You drop the reins and let them go. It's like being on a great roller coaster for the first time and putting your hands in the air; it's a little scary but such a great rush!

Here are a couple of ways to get at controlled chaos.

You give them group work- maybe doing research or finding answers in some text or setting up for a debate- Tell them directions, and just let them go. You will be able to tell they are working and having a good time doing it. You are the observer.

Another way is to have a class discussion where students take the lead from you and engage with each other in a productive, academic, and engaging debate/discussion with themselves. Socratic seminars can work this way.

The goal is for you to step back and observe them learning on their own.

Montessori does this extremely well. I've seen teachers use stations in class quite effectively as well. It's so much fun to watch!

They don't need you to "drive" them; they work together (don't forget to establish group norms prior to the work) to find their way. It is great to see them follow and adhere to group norms, allowing each other to be heard and not attacking each other personally but addressing their ideas.

This can happen two ways-

One, it can be set up beforehand and be part of a lesson. For example- they know they have a day to do in-class research to set up for a debate the next day.

Two, it can happen organically, you bring up a topic and the students run with it. They take you out of the equation by discussing amongst themselves. All you do is stand back to make sure norms are adhered to.

This is one of the most beautiful moments of teaching that can happen.

This is what you strive for — a classroom full of students learning from one another with you as their guide. Beautiful.

VI.

The transition from knowing how to teach to becoming a teacher is vital to your evolution.

There is no going back. You have made it this far.

We have had a long conversation about developing as a teacher but the vital aspect of this book is the separation of you as a teacher and you as a person.

Your soul should be the same inside and outside of the classroom.

Your "self" should be essentially the same.

The "I and the Teacher"

However.

Who you are inside the classroom is not who you are outside. What I mean is that you cannot be all consumed with being a teacher outside the classroom in your life.

There must be some separation or you will burn out. The fire will die.

Being a teacher is about progress, not perfection.

It is about customizing your craft and navigating through your first couple of years.

It is about developing a yearlong conversation with your students.

"The Long Conversation."

It is about being compassionate towards yourself and your students.

It is about being curious about the world and teaching your students that curiosity is the heart and soul of education.

It is about being prepared for everything that can happen in a class and positively reacting to the things you never thought would happen when they do.

It is about innovating and evolving both in your practice and your policies.

It is about being flexible and knowing that life, and teaching, ebb and flow like the waves in an ocean.

It is about being aware that cynicism and apathy slowly kills everything they touch.

It is about you recognizing your students and their gifts, inside and outside the classroom.

It is about being amazed and inspired by your students when you give them the voice and opportunity to become who they are.

It is about being aware of the amazing wonder our world offers and transferring that to students.

It is about engagement and inspiration.

It is about developing persistence, grit, and a work ethic for both you and your students.

It is about making decisions and having short-term and long-term goals. For both you and your life as a teacher.

It is about exploring and traveling the world.

It is about giving students access.

It is about creating equity

It is about a coupling of theory and practice.

It is about modeling behavior and attitude for students.

It is about being passionate about your favorite subject.

It is about smiling, laughing, and being excited daily.

It is about telling stories. The good kind, where you succeed and where you fail and how you learned from both.

It is about challenging yourself and your students, even if they get frustrated, annoyed, or even angry. Good.

It is about having fun and being authentic, both inside the classroom and outside in your life.

It is about changing lives. And all the students who come back to say, "Thank You."

It is about being exhausted at times, overwhelmed at times, and underwhelmed at times.

It is about asking questions and searching for answers.

It is about being kind and available when students need you. Knowing that you care about them is vital. Lending an ear, offering advice, and keeping them safe can change lives.

It is about connecting to the students, connecting to the skills and the content, connecting to the modern world and history, and is about creating a connection to EVERYTHING!

It is about the art and the craft.

V.

The goal is to get students to think, read, act, and connect critically in and around:

> Their world: local and global
> Information and arguments
> Media
> Literature, Science, Math, History
> Artistic pursuits
> Writing and speaking
> Themselves

You want to put a "ding in the universe" (Steve Jobs) or "make a difference" (Taylor Mali) or "change the paradigm" (Sir Ken Robinson).

You will as a teacher.

This is the greatest job in the world. And you GET to do it; you don't have to.

One of the great things about teaching is the students change every year. Your classes are never exactly the same.

Want a new challenge? Teach a new prep, change a grade level or a new population. That makes it a whole new adventure.

It's the greatest job ever and we are lucky to have the opportunity.

Remember, this is a profession, not a lifestyle- the I and the Teacher.

Teaching is a craft that needs to be navigated, practiced, and cultivated.

The fire burns brightly for those willing to light it, tend it, and stoke it.

The fire can burn for a long time if you want it to.

Customize your practice to ignite and inspire you and your students.

Build your craft

Follow your compass.

Good luck.

For additional sources, information, and the ability to work with Troy visit:

Compass Teacher Education at
www.compassteachered.com

Bio-

Troy Bradbury has been teaching for almost 20 years. Before transitioning into AP Capstone, Troy was an English teacher and AP Language and Composition teacher. He is the site-coordinator for the University of Maryland's College of Education Professional Develop School and a mentor teacher training both undergraduate students and graduate students. Dedicated to advancing global education and the promotion of 21st century skills, Troy has also been a part of various international teacher exchange programs including the World Affairs Council teacher exchange program in South Africa, the Teachers for Global Classrooms (IREX) exchange with Brazil, and the Japan Fulbright Memorial Fund exchange. He is also College Board Teacher Consultant for AP Seminar and a National Board Certified Teacher.

References

Chapter 2:

Slim, P. (2014). *Body of work: finding the thread that ties your story together.* New York: Portfolio/Penguin.

Chapter 3:

Godin, S. (2012). *Stop Stealing Dreams: (what is school for?).* Seth Godin.

Lancasterian Society. (n.d.). Retrieved September 09, 2017, from http://www.lancasterian.org/

Chapter 4:

Fulghum, R. (1997). *It was on fire when I lay down on it.* New York: Ballantine Books.

Chapter 7:

Ripley, A. (2014). *The smartest kids in the world: and how they got that way.* New York, NY: Simon & Schuster Paperbacks.

Wiggins, G. P., & McTighe, J. (2008). *Understanding by design.* Alexandria, VA: Association for Supervision and Curriculum Development.

Chapter 9:

Lee, H. (1960). *To Kill a Mockingbird.* New York, NY: Grand Central

Pressfield, S. (2012). *Turning Pro*. New York, NY: Black Irish.

Chapter 10:

Alfie Kohn- Home. (n.d.). Retrieved September 09, 2017, from http://www.alfiekohn.org/

Start With Why - Simon Sinek TED talk. (n.d.). Retrieved September 09, 2017, from https://ed.ted.com/on/Vt83VF0O

Wagner, T. (2014). *The global achievement gap: why even our best schools dont teach the new survival skills our children need--and what we can do about it*. New York: Basic Books.

Wagner, T., & Compton, R. A. (2015). *Creating innovators: the making of young people who will change the world*. New York, NY: Scribner.

Wagner, T., & Dintersmith, T. (2015). *Most likely to succeed: a new vision for education to prepare our kids for todays innovation economy*. New York, NY: Scribner.

Chapter 11:

Robinson, K. (n.d.). Changing education paradigms. Retrieved September 09, 2017, from https://www.ted.com/talks/ken_robinson_changing_education_paradigms

Mali, T. (n.d.). Taylor Mali. Retrieved September 09, 2017, from https://www.ted.com/speakers/taylor_mali

Made in the USA
Lexington, KY
01 December 2017